Essential Cryptography for JavaScript Developers

A practical guide to leveraging common cryptographic operations in Node.js and the browser

Alessandro Segala

BIRMINGHAM—MUMBAI

Essential Cryptography for JavaScript Developers

Copyright © 2022 Packt Publishing

Associate Group Product Manager: Rohit Rajkumar
Senior Editor: Keagan Carneiro
Content Development Editor: Divya Vijayan
Technical Editor: Simran Udasi
Copy Editor: Safis Editing
Project Coordinator: Rashika Ba
Proofreader: Safis Editing
Indexer: Subalakshmi Govindhan
Production Designer: Shyam Sundar Korumilli
Marketing Coordinator: Anamika Singh

First published: February 2022

Production reference: 1140122

Published by Packt Publishing Ltd.
Livery Place
35 Livery Street
Birmingham
B3 2PB, UK.

ISBN 978-1-80107-533-6

www.packt.com

*To my family and dearest friends; my girlfriend, Clare; my parents,
Maria Grazia and Francesco; and my brother, Christian, who, even during
these challenging times, have shown love and continued support to each other.*

– Alessandro Segala

Contributors

About the author

Alessandro Segala is a product manager at Microsoft working on developer tools. A software engineer at heart, he has over a decade of experience building full stack web applications, having worked as a professional developer as well as contributing to and maintaining various open source projects. In addition to writing about software development on his blog, Alessandro had his first book, *Svelte 3 Up and Running*, published by Packt in 2020.

About the reviewers

Deepal Jayasekara is a staff software engineer who is experienced in building large-scale, secure applications for payments, **infrastructure as a service (IaaS)**, and financial services industries. He writes and speaks about topics including JavaScript/Node.js, information security, and networking. He is also the founder of bibliocircle.com.

Justin Boyer is a tech enthusiast, self-proclaimed proud geek, and writer. He spent over 8 years in software development, focusing on CRM and web development technologies. He piloted the adoption of Node.js in his company and grew to appreciate its unique strengths. He later transitioned to application security, gaining his CSSLP and Security+ certifications and authoring several Pluralsight courses on appsec topics. He now works for himself, providing writing services to tech and cybersecurity companies, while keeping his tech chops current by volunteering his security expertise for a nonprofit and authoring more courses.

Josh Robinson is a code craftsman who thrives on cutting-edge technology. His love for coding began with the blue glow of a second hand Commodore 64 and has continued into his career building the future.

He can be stalked at *JoshRobinson* on Twitter and found creating new decentralized tech at bproto.io, where he is a founder.

Table of Contents

Part 2 – Using Common Cryptographic Operations with Node.js

3

File and Password Hashing with Node.js

4

Symmetric Encryption in Node.js

5

Using Asymmetric and Hybrid Encryption in Node.js

6

Digital Signatures with Node.js and Trust

Part 3 – Cryptography in the Browser

7

Introduction to Cryptography in the Browser

8

Performing Common Cryptographic Operations in the Browser

Index

Other Books You May Enjoy

Preface

The need for cryptography in application development is increasing steadily and goes hand-in-hand with the need to build solutions that better protect users' privacy and are safe even from more widespread, complex threats.

This book is designed to help software developers understand how to build common cryptographic operations as part of their solutions and to do so safely, using hashing, symmetric and asymmetric encryption, and digital signatures.

Throughout the book, we focus on the practical aspects that are relevant to all application developers, even those without a background in cryptography. For each class of cryptographic operation, we will learn about the role it plays in improving applications or unlocking new opportunities, which algorithms are commonly used, and what you need to know to be able to use it safely.

Written by a developer for developers, this book contains what I've learned over many years of working with cryptography and implementing applications based on common cryptographic schemes. I've made a conscious decision to skip formal explanations of *how* algorithms work, including the mathematical formulations behind them, and I'm instead focusing on practical, actionable knowledge that every developer can feel comfortable leveraging as part of the solutions they're building.

Who this book is for

This book is for software developers that don't necessarily have a background in cryptography yet have a curiosity in the topic and want to know how to leverage it as part of their solutions, correctly and safely.

Throughout the book, examples will be provided of code samples in JavaScript, running in a Node.js environment first and then inside browser-based applications. We chose JavaScript because of its potential to be used anywhere, from servers and browsers to desktop and mobile applications.

However, aside from the specific code samples, the concepts explained in this book – including the descriptions of the various cryptographic operations, what they're used for, and how they're used – are relevant to developers working with any programming language or framework.

What this book covers

Chapter 1, Cryptography for Developers, introduces the book by presenting the value that leveraging cryptography provides to developers, and then explains some core concepts used throughout all the chapters.

Chapter 2, Dealing with Binary and Random Data, demonstrates how binary data is managed in Node.js and how it is encoded to strings, as well as how to generate random sequences of bytes, all of which are operations frequently used when working with cryptography.

Chapter 3, File and Password Hashing with Node.js, is a practical overview of how to calculate digests of messages and files with Node.js with the SHA-2 family of functions, as well as how to hash passwords and derive keys with Argon2 and scrypt.

Chapter 4, Symmetric Encryption in Node.js, explains how to use symmetric ciphers such as AES and ChaCha20-Poly1305 with Node.js to encrypt messages and files.

Chapter 5, Using Asymmetric and Hybrid Encryption in Node.js, demonstrates using asymmetric cryptography to encrypt data with Node.js; this includes using RSA and hybrid encryption schemes based on RSA or Elliptic Curve Cryptography with ECIES.

Chapter 6, Digital Signatures with Node.js and Trust, includes both an introduction to calculating and verifying digital signatures with Node.js (using RSA or Elliptic Curve Cryptography) and an explanation of certificates and trust.

Chapter 7, Introduction to Cryptography in the Browser, explains the benefits and challenges of performing cryptography in the browser with JavaScript and includes an overview of dealing with binary and random data in frontend apps.

Chapter 8, Performing Common Cryptographic Operations in the Browser, demonstrates performing the cryptographic operations analyzed throughout the book in the context of apps running inside a web browser.

To get the most out of this book

All the code samples in this book are written in modern JavaScript, adopting syntax up to ES2017, including Promises and async/await. Nevertheless, the concepts presented in this book can be leveraged by developers working with other programming languages and frameworks, too.

In the first six chapters, we are assuming that all JavaScript code runs in a Node.js environment, for example, in a server-side application or using frameworks such as Electron. The minimum version of Node.js that is capable of running every code sample in this book is 15; however, we recommend using **Node.js 16** (the current LTS as of writing) or higher.

The last two chapters include JavaScript code that is meant to be executed inside a web browser, using APIs that are available in recent versions of all modern desktop and mobile browsers, including Chrome, Edge, Firefox, Safari, or another Chromium-based browser (notably, Internet Explorer is not supported). It's assumed that the code will be included in frontend applications packaged with a bundler such as Webpack, Rollup, or esbuild (the usage of those tools falls outside the scope of this book). More information on browser support and links to compatibility tables are included in the *Technical requirements* section of *Chapter 7, Introduction to Cryptography in the Browser*. For development and experimentation with frontend code, we have also provided a "playground" that can run inside a web browser: `https://bit.ly/crypto-playground`.

Software covered in the book	Operating system requirements
Node.js (16 or higher recommended)	Windows, macOS, or Linux
Modern JavaScript (ES2017)	
A modern web browser such as Chrome, Edge, Firefox, Safari, or another Chromium-based browser	

If you are using the digital version of this book, we advise you to type the code yourself or access the code from the book's GitHub repository (a link is available in the next section). Doing so will help you avoid any potential errors related to the copying and pasting of code.

Download the example code files

You can download the example code files for this book from GitHub at `https://bit.ly/crypto-gh`. If there's an update to the code, it will be updated in the GitHub repository.

We also have other code bundles from our rich catalog of books and videos available at `https://github.com/PacktPublishing/`. Check them out!

Download the color images

We also provide a PDF file that has color images of the screenshots and diagrams used in this book. You can download it here: `https://static.packt-cdn.com/downloads/9781801075336_ColorImages.pdf`.

Conventions used

There are a number of text conventions used throughout this book.

`Code in text`: Indicates code words in text, database table names, folder names, filenames, file extensions, pathnames, dummy URLs, user input, and Twitter handles. Here is an example: " We use the `decipher` object, just like we did with the cipher object in the previous method, invoking `decipher.update` with the ciphertext to decrypt and use `decipher.final` when we're done."

A block of code is set as follows:

```
const crypto = require('crypto')
const fs = require('fs')
const util = require('util')
const readFile = util.promisify(fs.readFile)
```

When we wish to draw your attention to a particular part of a code block, the relevant lines or items are set in bold:

```
const bobPublicKeyPem = bobKeyPair.publicKey.export(
    {type: 'spki', format: 'pem'}
)
const aliceSharedSecret = crypto.diffieHellman({
    publicKey: crypto.createPublicKey(bobPublicKeyPem),
    privateKey: aliceKeyPair.privateKey
})
```

Any command-line input or output is written as follows:

```
$ openssl genrsa -out private.pem 4096
```

Bold: Indicates a new term, an important word, or words that you see onscreen. For instance, words in menus or dialog boxes appear in **bold**. Here is an example: "Select **System info** from the **Administration** panel."

Tips or Important Notes
Appear like this.

Get in touch

Feedback from our readers is always welcome.

General feedback: If you have questions about any aspect of this book, email us at customercare@packtpub.com and mention the book title in the subject of your message.

Errata: Although we have taken every care to ensure the accuracy of our content, mistakes do happen. If you have found a mistake in this book, we would be grateful if you would report this to us. Please visit www.packtpub.com/support/errata and fill in the form.

Piracy: If you come across any illegal copies of our works in any form on the internet, we would be grateful if you would provide us with the location address or website name. Please contact us at copyright@packt.com with a link to the material.

If you are interested in becoming an author: If there is a topic that you have expertise in and you are interested in either writing or contributing to a book, please visit authors.packtpub.com.

Share Your Thoughts

Once you've read *Essential Cryptography for JavaScript Developers*, we'd love to hear your thoughts! Scan the QR code below to go straight to the Amazon review page for this book and share your feedback.

https://packt.link/r/1801075336

Your review is important to us and the tech community and will help us make sure we're delivering excellent quality content.

Part 1 – Getting Started

In this first section, we will begin with an overview of the main topics covered in this book, the various operations we're covering, and the core principles that will guide the rest of the book. We will then proceed to learn about how to work with binary and random data in Node.js, two common occurrences while working with cryptography.

This section comprises the following chapters:

- *Chapter 1, Cryptography for Developers*

- *Chapter 2, Dealing with Binary and Random Data*

1
Cryptography for Developers

"Dance like no one's watching. Encrypt like everyone is."

– Anonymous

Few things are as important for application security as cryptography. Done properly, it can make data unreadable to attackers even if you suffer a breach. But do it wrong, and it can actually amplify the impact of other vulnerabilities.

While cryptography is incredibly accessible to developers nowadays, many still have questions around how to use it, when to use it, and which of the many options or algorithms to pick.

This book will try to answer those questions without going into formal, academic explanations, and without complex mathematical formulas or diagrams, in a way that is friendly to developers. Unlike many other books on the topic, our goal won't be to train you to become a cryptographer. Instead, by the end of this book, you'll hopefully have enough knowledge of the most important algorithms to be able to use them in your code confidently.

All code samples in this book are written in **JavaScript** and assume a **Node.js** execution environment, with the exception of *Part 3, Cryptography in the browser, in which we'll look at the Web Crypto APIs for usage in a web browser*. However, even if you code in a different programming language, you will be able to follow along to learn the core concepts, and then replicate them in your preferred stack using one of the many libraries that are available to you.

In this first chapter, we're going to introduce the book and cover the following topics:

- An overview of what cryptography is and why it matters to developers
- A definition of "safe" in the context of cryptography
- Types and "layers" of encryption

What is cryptography and why should a developer care?

Cryptography is everywhere around us and it impacts directly or indirectly on every aspect of our lives, every day, even when you don't notice it.

Cryptography is used to protect the information we share on the internet. You'll also find it when you're authenticating yourself to use your phone or laptop, or swiping the badge to get into your office. Cryptography is used to secure every digital payment transaction and to guarantee contracts that are signed digitally. It is also used to protect data we store on our devices, both from unauthorized access and from accidental corruption.

Protecting secrets...

Most people, even those who are not particularly tech-savvy, know that cryptography as the science and practice of protecting messages, files, and data, such as by encrypting and decrypting them.

In fact, this use of cryptography, to shield messages from adversaries, is thousands of years old. A common example is the *Caesar cipher* (a **cipher** is an algorithm used for encryption or decryption), which is named after the Roman emperor Julius Caesar; this is a classic example of a "substitution cipher," in which letters of the alphabet are substituted with one another. In the case of the Caesar cipher, each letter was shifted by three, so the letter A became D, B became E, Z became C, and so on.

Other famous historical ciphers include the *Vigenère cipher*, which in the 16th century first introduced the concept of an "encryption key," and then mechanical ones such as the Enigma machine, used by Nazi Germany during World War II and eventually broken by Polish and English researchers (this was also the topic of the 2014 movie *The Imitation Game*, which depicted the work of Alan Turing and the other researchers at Bletchley Park).

While the history of cryptography can be an interesting topic per se, and it provides invaluable lessons on common types of attacks against cryptography, all those historical ciphers are considered broken and so are not useful to modern application developers. As such, we won't be spending more time talking about them in this book, but nevertheless, I encourage curious readers to learn more about them!

…and the other uses of modern cryptography

Despite the strong association with ensuring confidentiality and hiding secrets, modern cryptography is used for much more than that.

In fact, throughout this book, we'll be using cryptographic functions for a variety of purposes, some of which are meant to be shared with the public rather than kept as secrets:

- In *Chapter 3, File and Password Hashing with Node.js*, we'll learn about hashing, which is a one-way cryptographic operation that allows you to derive a fixed-length digest for any message. This is used for purposes including checking the integrity of files or messages, generating identifiers and encryption keys, and protecting passwords.

- In *Chapter 4, Symmetric Encryption in Node.js*, and *Chapter 5, Using Asymmetric and Hybrid Encryption in Node.js*, we'll look at data encryption and decryption using various kinds of ciphers.

- In *Chapter 6, Digital Signatures with Node.js and Trust*, we'll learn how cryptography can be used to create and validate digital signatures, which can be used (among other things) to authenticate the author of a message, certifying its provenance, or preventing repudiation.

Why this matters to developers

As a software developer, understanding the practices presented above can help you build applications that implement cryptographic operations safely, using the most appropriate solutions. There are many possible uses of cryptography, and the aforementioned list contains only some examples.

Not all the operations we're going to learn about in this book will be useful or even relevant for every application you might be working on. However, the topics presented in the next chapters are possibly the most common ones, which developers can leverage to solve frequent real-world problems.

In fact, given the current state of application development, nowadays you could argue that knowing how to safely implement the solutions described in this book should be a skill most developers need to be at least somehow familiar with, without the need to consult with expert cryptographers.

Globally, cyberattacks have been getting more and more frequent every year and are carried out by increasingly more sophisticated adversaries, sometimes including state-sponsored actors. Just as attacks have increased in both quantity and quality, thanks to the pervasiveness of digital systems in our businesses and lives, the impact of breaches has grown costlier, with damage that can be in the range of millions of dollars and, in certain cases, catastrophic or fatal.

Whereas security used to be an afterthought in the software development life cycle, at times relegated to an issue for operations specialists only, teams are now tasked with considering it during every stage of the development process. Many organizations are also adopting practices such as DevSecOps and "shift left security," in which the security needs of an entire solution are included in the entire software development life cycle, from planning and development to operations.

DevOps and DevSecOps

DevOps is a set of principles and practices, aided by specialized tools, to enable the continuous delivery of value to end users. DevOps is built around practices such as **Continuous Integration** (**CI**) and **Continuous Delivery** (**CD**), agile software development, and continuous monitoring that are meant to bring the development and operations teams closer together and allow faster application release cycles, and continuous learning and improvement.

To learn more about DevOps, visit `https://bit.ly/crypto-devops`

Building on DevOps, **DevSecOps** requires the integration of security practices and thinking into every stage of the DevOps process – planning, building, delivering, and operating. Organizations that adopt DevSecOps believe that security is a shared responsibility among every person and team that has any dealing with an application.

To learn more about DevSecOps, visit
`https://bit.ly/crypto-devsecops`

For example, whereas corporate or **Local Networks (LANs)** were traditionally considered safe, it's now common practice to assume your systems have been breached and practice **defense in depth** or add multiple layers of protection. So, an application that encrypts data in transit prevents an eavesdropper (called a **Man-in-the-Middle** or **MitM**) from potentially stealing secrets, even inside a LAN.

It should go without saying that while adding cryptography to your applications is often necessary to make them safe, it's almost always not sufficient. For example, protecting your users' data with strong encryption will help limit the impact of breaches but will be useless against account takeovers through social engineering.

Nevertheless, cryptography does play an important role in the process of protecting data; for example, it secures the data your application uses (both at rest and in transit), ensuring the integrity of the information stored or exchanged, authenticating end users or other services, preventing tampering, and so on.

In addition to learning about the different classes of cryptographic operations that you can take advantage of, with this book I also hope you will be equipped to understand when to use each one in the safest way possible.

In fact, just as not using cryptography can lead to serious consequences, implementing cryptography in the wrong way can be equally as bad. This can happen when developers use broken algorithms (for this reason, we'll be sticking to a few tried-and-tested ones in this book) or buggy implementations of good algorithms, such as libraries containing security vulnerabilities (which is why we're going to recommend built-in standard libraries whenever possible). In other cases, issues could be caused by developers picking the wrong cryptographic operations; one too-common example is storing passwords in databases that have been encrypted with a symmetric cipher rather than hashed, as we'll see later in the book.

Lastly, I would like to point out that the five classes of cryptographic operations we're covering in this book do not represent all the different algorithms and protocols that can be used by modern applications, nor all the possible different uses of cryptography.

For example, end-to-end encrypted messaging apps or VPNs often need to implement special key exchange algorithms, or full-disk encryption apps may leverage different algorithms or modes of operation than the ones we'll be looking at. Such problems tend to be more specific to a certain domain or type of application, and if you are building a solution that requires them, you might need to perform some additional research or work with a cryptographer.

What this book is about – and what it's not

This book is about the practical uses of common cryptographic operations that software developers without a background in cryptography can leverage.

In each chapter, we'll present a specific class of cryptographic operations, and for each, we'll then look at the following:

- What it's used for and what it should not be used for.
- What the most common algorithms are that developers should use.
- Considerations on what parameters to set for using the algorithms safely, when appropriate.
- Lastly, we'll look at sample code implementing the specific algorithms, written in JavaScript for execution on Node.js (with a nod to cryptography in the browser in the last two chapters).

Just as we have covered what this book is about, it's important to also mention what this book is *not* about, listing four things that you will not be learning in the following chapters:

- First, this book is not about *how* cryptographic algorithms work, or a description of the algorithms themselves.

  As we've mentioned many times already, our book's goal is not to train cryptographers but rather to help developers build better applications leveraging common cryptographic algorithms. In this book, you will not encounter formal descriptions of the algorithms and their flows, the mathematical models behind them, and so on.

- Second, following on from the previous point, we will be looking at how to *use* cryptographic algorithms and not at how to *implement* them.

  The latter not only requires a deep understanding of how algorithms work but is also a dangerous minefield because of the risks associated with poor implementations. At the risk of sounding hyperbolic, an entire class of attacks could be made possible by doing things as common as using `if` statements in code implementing a cryptographic algorithm.

  In short, we'll leave the implementation to the experts, and we'll stick to using pre-built libraries. Whenever possible, that will be the built-in standard library of Node.js.

- Third, as mentioned previously, this book is about strong, modern cryptography only. We'll focus on a limited set of widely adopted algorithms and functions that have been "battle-tested" and are generally deemed *safe* by cryptographers (more on what "safe" means in the next section). Simple or historical ciphers, codes, and so on might be interesting to those wanting to learn the science of cryptography or looking for brain-teasers, but are of little practical relevance for our goal.

- Fourth, we will not be talking about the other kind of "crypto", that is, *cryptocurrencies*. While Bitcoin, Ethereum, and the like are indeed based on the blockchain technology, which makes extensive use of cryptography (especially hashing and digital signatures), that's where the commonality ends. Nevertheless, should you be interested in learning about how blockchains work in the future, the concepts you'll learn from this book will likely be of use to you.

Rules of engagement

Lastly, before we begin, it's important to point out that cryptography is hard; making mistakes is surprisingly easy, and finding them can be really challenging. This is true even for expert cryptographers!

You'll often hear two very strong recommendations that are meant to keep you and the applications you're building safe. If you allow me, I propose that we turn them into a kind of "Hippocratic oath," which I invite you to repeat after me:

1. *I will not invent my own cryptographic algorithms.*
2. *I will not roll my own implementation of cryptographic algorithms.*

Thankfully for us, a lot of very brilliant cryptographers have worked for decades to design strong algorithms and implement them correctly and safely. As developers, the best thing we can do is to stick to proven, tested algorithms, and leverage existing, audited libraries to adopt them. Normally, that means using whatever is available on the **standard library** of the language you're using, the APIs exposed by the operating system or runtime environment, or leveraging **well-known, audited libraries**.

As we've now introduced the topic and the goals of this book, and hopefully convinced you of the importance of adopting cryptography in your applications, we're now ready to get started with our learning, starting with setting some shared understanding.

Defining "safe"

An important concept when we deal with cryptography is to define what "safe" means in this context.

As a rule of thumb, possibly **every cryptographic algorithm can be broken, given a sufficient amount of computing power and time**.

For simplicity, we'll focus the next examples on data encryption, although the same would apply to all other classes of cryptographic operations.

The goal of using cryptography is to make sure that the effort (computing power multiplied by time) is too big for an attacker to attempt to break your encryption. Assuming that the algorithms you use do not have flaws in their design or backdoors that can be exploited, the only way attackers can crack your encryption is by doing a brute-force attack.

A **brute-force attack** works by trying every single combination possible until you find the right one. For example, if you were trying to break a padlock with 3 digits, each from 0 to 9, you'd have 1,000 different combinations (000, 001, 002… until 999), and the correct one would be one of those. On average, it would take you 500 attempts before you could find the right one (the number of possible permutations divided by 2). If every attempt takes you 3 seconds to try, then you can expect to be done in 1,500 seconds on average, or 25 minutes.

In theory, brute force *can* break any encryption. The goal is to use encryption that is strong enough to make it impractical to break it using a brute-force attack.

For example, AES-128 (a symmetric cipher) uses a 128-bit key, which means that there are 2^{128} possible combinations, or 340,282,366,920,938,463,463,374,607,431,768,211,456; that is, approximately 3.4×10^{38}. That is a *very* large number that ought to be put into perspective.

Getting Perspective

One of the largest computing grids in the world today, if perhaps not *the* largest, is the network of all the Bitcoin mining grids. In 2021, the Bitcoin network reached an estimated peak hash rate of 180 million terahashes per second, which would translate to being able to compute about 2^{92} hashes per year. This is a metric that is commonly used to indicate how much compute power is being used by the network.

Imagine a hypothetical scenario in which all Bitcoin miners agreed to get together and convert the entire grid to brute-force a 128-bit key. If they managed to attempt 2^{92} keys per year, it would still take them an average of 2^{35} years, or over 10^{10} years, to complete the attack (2^{128} possible keys, divided by 2^{92} keys attempted per year, divided by 2 to get the average time). That's roughly the same as the age of the universe, which is estimated to be around 14 billion years old, or about 10^{10}.

Of course, computing power increases constantly, so the time it will take to break cryptography in the future will be less.

Quantum computing will also make it easier to break certain kinds of cryptography, although those systems are still experimental today and not yet powerful enough for most practical applications (nevertheless, cryptographers are already preparing for that future today, by designing stronger "post-quantum" algorithms).

That said, our goal should always be to choose algorithms that are guaranteed to protect our data for at least **as long as it's necessary**. For example, let's say you encrypt a document containing the password of your online banking account today; if technological innovation allowed an attacker to crack it in "only" 100 years from now, it might not matter to you at that point, as you'll most likely be dead by then.

Given the aforementioned context, **an algorithm should be considered "broken" when it's possible to crack it in a way that is significantly faster than using a brute-force attack**.

Most cryptographic algorithms that we use today are safe in this sense because the only possible attacks against them are brute-force ones, which as we've seen are just not practical.

How Cryptography Is Broken – the Example of Frequency Analysis

At the beginning of this chapter, we looked at some historical ciphers and explained that they were broken. Substitution ciphers are among the oldest and simplest ones, and they rely on replacing every letter of the alphabet with another one. For example, in the Caesar cipher, letters are shifted by three, so A is replaced with D, B with E, and so on. While this may have been effective to protect messages from the illiterate enemy soldiers of the era, it looks trivial today.

Substitution ciphers that rely on the shifting of letters can be broken in a fairly simple way with brute-force attacks, even manually (assuming, of course, that the attacker knows that the cipher works by shifting letters). With only 26 letters in the English alphabet, it takes at most 25 attempts to find the number by which characters are shifted.

A more complex substitution cipher could instead create a new alphabet in which letters are randomly shuffled. So, the letter A may be replaced with X, B with C, and D with P. With the English alphabet, there are 26! (26 factorial) possible combinations, or about 10^{26}, offering a decent amount of protection against brute-force attacks, even against an adversary that can use modern computers.

However, through cryptanalysis (the science of studying cryptographic systems looking for weaknesses), even those more "advanced" substitution ciphers have been broken, through a technique called *frequency analysis*. This works by looking at the frequency of letters (and pairs of letters) in the encrypted text and comparing that with the average frequency of letters in English writing. For example, "E" is the most frequently used letter in English text, so whatever letter is the most used in the encrypted text will likely correspond to "E."

While cryptanalysis is certainly not something we'll focus on in this book, this mention will hopefully provide an insight into one of the (many) ways algorithms can be broken.

With an understanding of how encryption helps protect data and a contextualization of what it means for data to be "safe," we now need to look at the multiple ways that data can be encrypted.

Types and "layers" of encryption

Before we begin talking about data encryption throughout this book, we should clarify the various types of data encryption and the layers at which data can be encrypted.

First, with regards to types, it's useful to distinguish between these three:

1. **Encryption at rest** refers to the practice of encrypting data when it's stored on a persistent medium. Some canonical examples include storing files in an encrypted hard drive or turning on data encryption for your database systems. When data is encrypted at rest, it's protected against certain kinds of attacks, such as physical ones on the computers/servers that store the data (for example, stolen hard drives). However, data is usually decrypted in-memory while it's being processed, so attackers that manage to infiltrate a live system may have the ability to steal your data as plaintext.

   For example, it's common nowadays to encrypt the hard drives of computers, which is especially important to prevent people from reading data from the storage of a laptop that is lost or stolen. However, while the laptop is powered on, the encryption keys are present in memory (RAM), so malicious applications running on the system may get full access to everything stored on the hard drive.

2. **Encryption in transit** refers to the practice of encrypting data while it's being transmitted over an untrusted channel. The most common example is **Transport Layer Security** (**TLS**), used by the HTTPS protocol for securing access to websites; this protects the information exchanged between a client and web server over the internet (for example, passwords or other sensitive data). In this case, a MitM that managed to tap the wire would not be able to see the actual data being exchanged. However, both the client that sends the data and the server that receives it are able to see the message in plaintext.

3. **End-to-end encryption** (also called **E2E Encryption** or **E2EE**) is the practice of encrypting a client's data before sending it to a remote server so that only the client has the keys to decrypt it. This is commonly used with cloud storage; your documents are encrypted on your laptop before being sent to the cloud provider, and the keys never leave your laptop. The cloud provider sees only encrypted blobs of data and cannot read what you're storing on their service or do any processing on that data (although they might still gather insights based on metadata, such as the size of the encrypted blobs; for example, encrypted videos are much larger than encrypted photos!).

The techniques we're going to learn in this book will primarily apply to developers building solutions for encrypting data at rest or that leverage end-to-end encryption. For most applications that require encryption in transit, developers will find it much more efficient (and effective) to leverage algorithms such as TLS (HTTPS) as proven and universal standards.

Secondly, it's also worth pointing out that encryption can be layered, meaning that data can be encrypted multiple times to provide greater protection against attackers:

- Data can be encrypted with multiple layers of the same encryption type. For example, you might encrypt a file you're working on (for example, using PGP (Pretty Good Privacy)/GPG (GNU Privacy Guard), or creating an encrypted ZIP file) and store that on an encrypted hard drive. Both operations provide encryption at rest for the data, yet they serve different purposes; encrypting the file makes it so an attacker with access to the running system could not see its contents, while the full-disk encryption ensures that someone stealing your laptop could not even see that the encrypted file exists in there (not even its filename in many cases).

- Data can also be encrypted with multiple types of encryptions. For example, you could be storing a file protected with end-to-end encryption on a remote server and use TLS (encryption in transit) while transmitting it. While this wouldn't give you more protection against eavesdroppers trying to read what data you're sending, it can offer additional privacy because they would not be able to see that information is being sent to the cloud storage provider in the first place.

Layered encryption is especially common in the context of in-transit data encryption. For example, when you connect to the internet through a Wi-Fi network that is secured with a password (for example, using the WPA2 protocol) and then visit a website over a secure HTTPS connection, your data in transit is encrypted twice: TLS (HTTPS) protects your communication between the laptop and the web server, and WPA2 offers additional protection between your laptop and the Wi-Fi access point.

Understanding the different types and layers of encryption is useful when you're designing your solution, as it allows you to identify where you should leverage cryptography to protect your and your users' data. This decision needs to be influenced by your solution's needs and your **threat model** (for more information, visit the OWASP page on threat modeling: `https://bit.ly/crypto-threat-modeling`).

Summary

In this first chapter, we have introduced the goal of this book – to provide practical foundations of cryptography for software developers. Then, we listed the concepts we'll be learning in the next chapters. We've also learned why developers should care about cryptography and discussed some best practices that people dealing with cryptography should follow as safeguards.

In the next chapter, we'll begin writing code, first by learning about how to deal with binary data in Node.js and how to encode that as text strings. We'll also look at how to generate random data with Node.js, something that we'll do frequently throughout this book.

2
Dealing with Binary and Random Data

When building solutions that leverage cryptography, we're almost always faced with two issues.

The first is managing **binary data**, which is a sequence of bytes, including characters that can't be represented as text. Most people have the experience of opening a *binary file* (such as an image and an executable application) in a text editor such as Notepad and being presented with a sequence of random, garbled symbols that can't be read, let alone edited.

In cryptography, encrypted messages, hashes, keys, and sometimes even decrypted messages are guaranteed to contain non-printable, binary data. This introduces challenges for developers as binary data often requires special handling to be visualized (such as while debugging our applications), stored, and transferred.

In this chapter, we'll explore how we can use encodings such as **base64** and **hex** (short for **hexadecimal**) with Node.js to make binary data representable as text so that it can be more easily dealt with.

The second issue we'll explore is generating **random data**. Random byte sequences are frequently used in cryptography, as we'll see throughout the book, including as encryption keys, seeds, and salts. Understanding how to generate them with Node.js is a very important part of building applications that leverage cryptography safely.

In this chapter, we'll explore:

- How to encode and represent binary data as hex or base64 with Node.js. We'll also include a primer on character encodings such as ASCII and UTF-8.
- How to generate cryptographically safe random byte sequences in Node.js.

Encoding and representing binary data

When using cryptography, including hashes, signatures, and encrypted messages, we commonly have to deal with binary data. As every developer has experienced while working with binary data or files, they cannot easily be printed on screen or copied and pasted into other fields, so it's common to change their representation by encoding them into strings that only use human-readable characters.

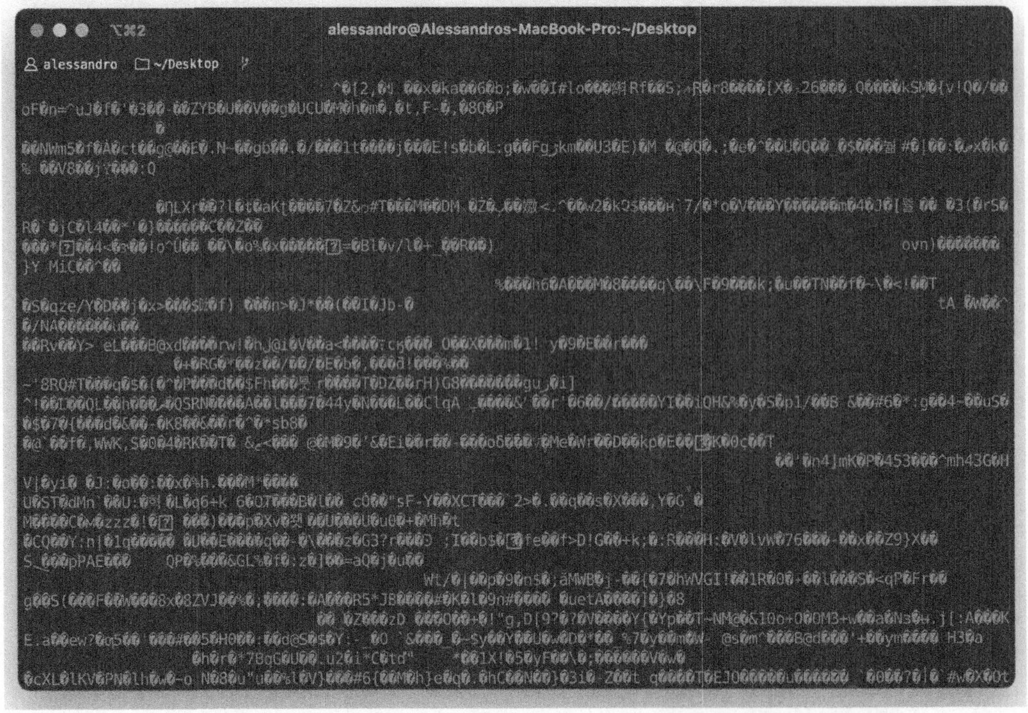

Figure 2.1 – Looking at binary data on a terminal. Note how the terminal is trying to interpret every byte sequence as UTF-8 and frequently encounters invalid ones (replaced with the "�" symbol)

In Node.js, binary data is generally stored in `Buffer` objects and can be represented in multiple ways, including some encodings that are guaranteed to be human-readable. Throughout this book, we'll frequently use two ways of representing binary data: **hex** (short for "hexadecimal", which uses base16) and **base64** encodings.

As we'll explain in a bit, encoded strings are always longer than the original, binary data, so they're generally not recommended for storing on a persistent storage medium (for example, in a database or a file on disk). However, unlike binary blobs, they have the advantage of being just sequences of printable ASCII characters. Representations such as hex or base64 make it possible for humans to analyze binary data much more easily, and they are simpler to transfer: they can be copied between different fields or systems more easily than binary data, including through copying and pasting.

A brief word on character encodings and why we encode binary data

Before we dive into ways of representing binary data, it helps to have a refresher on character encodings, including ASCII and UTF-8, as we'll be dealing with them often in this book.

Binary data is made of bytes, which, in modern computer systems, are sequences of 8 bits (each one either 0 or 1). This means that each byte can represent a number from 0 to 255 (2^8-1).

For computers to be able to display text, we have created **encodings**, which are conventions for converting between numbers and characters so that each character maps to a decimal number, and vice-versa.

One of the first such conventions that is still relevant today is **ASCII encoding** (American Standard Code for Information Interchange), which contains 128 symbols represented by a 7-bit number, 0 to 127 (this was before 8-bit systems became the standard they are today). The ASCII table includes the Latin alphabet with both lowercase and uppercase letters, numbers, some basic punctuation symbols, and other non-printable characters (things such as newlines, the tab character, and other control characters). For example, in the ASCII table, the number 71 would map to the character G (uppercase Latin g), and 103 would be g (lowercase Latin g).

> ASCII Table
>
> You can find a full list of the characters in the ASCII table online, for example, at `https://www.asciitable.xyz/`.

Throughout the years, other character encodings have been created, some of which found more adoption than others. However, one important development was the creation of the Unicode standard and its parent consortium, whose mission is to create a comprehensive encoding system to represent every character used by every alphabet around the world, and then more, including symbols, ligatures, and emojis. The Unicode standard contains a growing list of symbols. As of the time of writing, the current version is Unicode 14.0 and it contains almost 145,000 characters.

In addition to defining the list of symbols, Unicode also contains a few different character encodings. Among those, **UTF-8** is by far the most frequently used encoding on the Internet. It can represent each symbol of the Unicode standard by using between 1 and 4 bytes per character.

With UTF-8, the first 128 symbols are mapped exactly as in the ASCII table, so the ASCII table is essentially a "subset" of UTF-8 now. For symbols that are not defined in the ASCII table, including all non-Latin scripts, UTF-8 requires between 2 and 4 total bytes to represent them.

> **Use of UTF-8 in Code Samples**
>
> Throughout the code samples in this book, when dealing with text, we'll always assume that it is encoded as UTF-8: you'll often see us using methods that convert a Node.js `Buffer` object into a text string by requesting its UTF-8 representation. However, if your source data uses a different encoding (such as UTF-16 or another one), you will be able to modify your code to support that.

The problem with binary data, such as encrypted messages, is that they can contain any sequence of bytes, each one from 0 to 255, which, when interpreted as ASCII-encoded or UTF-8-encoded text, always contain a mix of unprintable characters and/or invalid sequences of bytes as per the UTF-8 standard. Thus, to be able to look at those strings conveniently, for ease of transmission or debugging, we need to represent the text in alternate forms, such as hex or base64.

Buffers in Node.js

In Node.js, binary data is commonly stored in `Buffer` objects. Many methods of the standard library that deal with binary data, including those in the `crypto` module that we'll be studying in this book, leverage buffers extensively.

There are multiple ways to create a `Buffer` object in Node.js. The two most important ones for now are the following:

- `Buffer.alloc(size)`, which allows the creation of an empty buffer of `size` bytes, by default, all zeros:

```
const buf = Buffer.alloc(3)
console.log(buf)
// -> <Buffer 00 00 00>
```

- `Buffer.from(*)` creates a `Buffer` object from a variety of sources, including arrays and `ArrayBuffer` objects, other `Buffer` objects, and, most importantly for us, strings.

When creating a buffer from a string, you can specify two arguments: `Buffer.from(string, encoding)`, where `encoding` is optional and defaults to `'utf8'` for UTF-8-encoded text (we'll see more encodings in the next pages of this chapter).

For example, these two statements instantiate a buffer with identical content:

```
const buf = Buffer.from('Hello world!', 'utf8')
const buf = Buffer.from('Hello world!')
```

Once created, `Buffer` objects contain a variety of properties and methods, some of which we'll encounter throughout this book. For now, it's worth highlighting two of them:

- `buf.toString(encoding)` is a method that returns the string representation of the buffer in the specified encoding (which defaults to `'utf8'` if not set); see this, for example:

```
const buf = Buffer.from('Hello world!', 'utf8')
console.log(buf.toString('utf8'))
// -> 'Hello world!'
```

In the preceding code, `buf.toString('utf8')` would have been identical to `buf.toString()`.

- `buf.length` is a property that contains the length of the buffer, in bytes; see this, for example:

```
const buf = Buffer.from('Hello world!', 'utf8')
console.log(buf.length)
// -> 12
```

Multi-Byte Characters in Unicode

Note that as per our discussion regarding encodings, some strings encoded as UTF-8 or UTF-16 may contain multi-byte characters, so their byte length can be different from their string length (or character count). For example, the letter è (Latin e with a grave) is displayed as a single character but uses two bytes when encoded as UTF-8, so:

`'è'.length` returns 1 because it counts the number of characters (here defined as Unicode code points).

`(Buffer.from('è', 'utf8')).length` returns 2 instead because the letter è in UTF-8 is encoded using two bytes.

If you're interested in learning more about character encodings, multi-byte characters, and the related topic of Unicode string normalization, I recommend the article *What every JavaScript developer should know about Unicode*, by Dmitri Pavlutin: `https://bit.ly/crypto-unicode`.

> **Buffer in Node.js**
>
> Full documentation for the `Buffer` APIs in Node.js can be found at
> `https://nodejs.org/api/buffer.html`.

Hex encoding

The first common way of representing binary data is to encode it in hexadecimal (hex for short) format.

With hex encoding, we split all bytes into two groups of 4 bits each, each able to represent 16 combinations, with numbers from 0 to 15 (2^4-1). Then we use a simplified encoding in which the first 10 combinations are represented by the numbers 0-9, and the remaining 6 use the letters a-f (case-insensitive).

Decimal	0 to 9	10	11	12	13	14	15
Hex	0 to 9	A or a	B or b	C or c	D or d	E or e	F or f

For example, the number 180 (`10110100` in binary) is outside of the bounds of the ASCII table (which only defines characters 0-127) and is not a valid sequence in UTF-8, so it can't be represented with either encoding. When encoded as hex, we are splitting that into two sequences of 4 bytes each: `1011` (11 in decimal, which maps to the letter B in the table above) and `0100` (4 in decimal). In hex, then, the representation of 180 is `B4`.

As you can see, when using hex encoding, the length of data in bytes doubles: while the number 180 can be stored in a single byte (which is not a printable character), writing `B4` in a file requires storing 2 characters, so 2 bytes.

You can encode any arbitrary byte sequence using hex. For example, the string `Hello world!` is represented as `48 65 6C 6C 6F 20 77 6F 72 6C 64 21` (for ease of reading, the convention is to use spaces to separate each byte, or every 2 characters encoded as hex; however, that's not mandatory). Multiple tools allow you to convert from ASCII or UTF-8 text to hex, such as `https://bit.ly/crypto-hex`. These tools can be used to perform the opposite operation too, as long as the data contains printable characters when decoded: as an example, try converting `48 65 B4 6C 6F` (note the B4 byte, which we observed previously as unprintable) into UTF-8, and you'll see that your computer will recognize an invalid UTF-8 sequence and display a "�" character to alert you to an error.

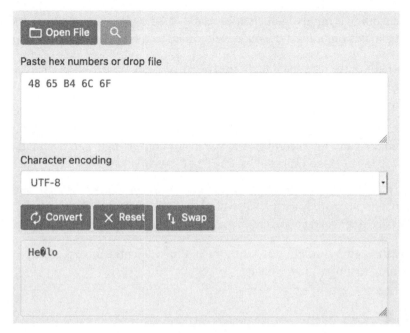

Figure 2.2 – Certain byte sequences such as B4 cannot be represented as UTF-8 text

With Node.js, you can create `Buffer` objects directly from hex-encoded strings, using the `Buffer.from` method with `'hex'` as encoding; the hex-encoded input is case-insensitive; see this, for example (note that spaces are not allowed between octets in the hex-encoded string for this method):

```
const buf = Buffer.from('48656C6C6F20776F726C6421', 'hex')
console.log(buf.toString('utf8'))
// -> 'Hello world!'
```

Likewise, you can use the `buf.toString('hex')` method to get the hex-encoded representation of any `Buffer` object, regardless of how it was created or whether it contains binary or textual data; see the following, for example:

```
const buf = Buffer.from('Hi, Buffer!', 'utf8')
console.log(buf.toString('hex'))
// -> '48692c2042756666657221'
```

Many programming languages, JavaScript included, allow you to write numbers in your code directly using their hexadecimal notation by adding the `0x` prefix. For example, the following expression in JavaScript prints `true`:

```
console.log(0xB4 === 180) // -> true
```

While hex encoding is highly inefficient in terms of storage requirements, as it doubles the size of our data, it is often used during development as it has three interesting properties:

- The length of the original data is always exactly half the length of the hex-encoded string.

- Each byte is represented by exactly two characters, and it's possible to convert them to decimal with a quick multiplication and addition: multiply the first character by 16, and then add the second (for example, for converting C1 to decimal, remember that C maps to 12, so the result is 12 * 16 + 1 = 193).

- If the data you've encoded is plain text, each sequence of two hex-encoded characters can map directly to a symbol in the ASCII table. For example, 41 in hex (65 in decimal) corresponds to the letter A (uppercase Latin a)

While these three things might not seem much, they can come in very handy when debugging code that uses binary data!

Base64

The second common way of representing binary data is base64. As the name suggests, this uses an encoding with 64 different symbols, each one representing 6 bits of the underlying data.

Just like hex encoding splits the underlying data into groups of 4 bits and then maps them to a small subset of symbols (16 in total), base64 uses groups of 6 bits and a set of 64 symbols. There are multiple character sets and specifications for base64 encoding, but the most common ones are as follows:

- The "Base64 standard encoding," as defined by RFC 4648 Section 4, uses the following 64 symbols:

```
ABCDEFGHIJKLMNOPQRSTUVWXYZabcdefghijklmnopqrstuvwxyz01234
56789+/
```

- The "Base64 URL encoding," as defined by RFC 4648 Section 5, uses the following 64 symbols:

```
ABCDEFGHIJKLMNOPQRSTUVWXYZabcdefghijklmnopqrstuvwxyz01234
56789-_
```

The two encodings are very similar (and, unlike hex, these are **case-sensitive**), but they differ in the symbols used to encode the decimal numbers 62 and 63, respectively, +/ for "standard encoding" and -_ for "URL encoding." In fact, many web applications prefer to use the second format because the characters + and / are not URL-safe, so they have to be encoded when used in a URL with the usual percentage encoding, becoming %2B and %2F, respectively. Instead, - and _ are URL-safe and do not require encoding when used in URLs.

Additionally, sometimes up to 2 padding characters, =, are added to make the length of base64-encoded strings an exact multiple of 4. Depending on the variant of base64 used and the parser library, padding may be required (base64-encoded strings that lack the required padding may not be parsed correctly) or optional (parsers accept strings with or without padding).

As you can already understand, base64 encoding is a bit more complex than the hex one, and we won't get into the details of the specifications or the algorithms for encoding and decoding strings with base64.

The good news is that Node.js supports base64 encoding natively in the Buffer APIs, with `'base64'` and `'base64url'` available as values for the encoding arguments in the methods we saw previously (note that `'base64url'` was added in Node.js 15.7); see this, for example:

```
const buf1 = Buffer.from('SGk=', 'base64')
console.log(buf1.toString())
// -> 'Hi'
const buf2 = Buffer.from('8424bff8', 'hex')
console.log(buf2.toString('base64'))
// -> 'hCS/+A=='
console.log(buf2.toString('base64url'))
// -> 'hCS_-A'
```

When using Node.js, note the following:

- All methods that parse a base64-encoded string (such as `Buffer.from`) accept base64-encoded data in any form, regardless of whether you're specifying `'base64'` or `'base64url'` as encoding, with optional padding. This means that the first line of the preceding code sample could have accepted input encoded with base64 in both "standard encoding" and "URL encoding," and using `'base64'` or `'base64url'` would not make a difference in either case. Additionally, with these methods, padding is always optional.

- Methods that format a string, encoding it with base64, use "standard encoding" when passing `'base64'` as the encoding format (and include padding if necessary), and "URL encoding" when passing `'base64url'` (never using padding), as you can see from the preceding code sample in the calls to `buf.toString(encoding)`.

While Node.js is fairly flexible with accepting base64-encoded input that uses either format, other applications, frameworks, or programming languages might not be. Especially when you're passing base64-encoded data between different applications or systems, be mindful to use the correct format!

Base64 URL Encoding in Older Versions of Node.js

As mentioned, `'base64url'` was implemented in Node.js 15.7. This has not changed the behavior of methods such as `Buffer.from`, which were accepting base64-encoded strings in either format before. However, methods such as `buf.toString()` only supported encoding to base64 in "standard encoding" format.

With Node.js < 15.7, encoding data from a `Buffer` object to URL-safe base64 required a few extra steps, such as this code, which might not be the prettiest but does the job:

```
buf.toString('base64')
  .replace(/=/g, '')
  .replace(/\+/g, '-')
  .replace(/\//g, '_')
```

Despite being quite a bit more complex, and trickier when mixing encoding standards and implementations, base64 is very useful because it's a more storage-efficient encoding than hex, yet it still relies entirely on printable characters in the ASCII table: encoding data using base64 generates strings that are just around 33% larger than the original binary data. Base64 is also widely supported, and it's used by data exchange formats such as JSON and XML when embedding binary data.

Now that we're comfortable with dealing with binary data, let's dive into the first situation (of the many in this book) in which we'll have to manage non-text sequences: generating random bytes.

Generating cryptographically secure random byte sequences

When building applications that leverage cryptography, it's very common to have to generate random byte sequences, and we'll encounter that in every chapter of this book. For example, we'll use random byte sequences as encryption keys (as in *Chapter 4, Symmetric Encryption in Node.js*) and as salt for hashes (*Chapter 3, File and Password Hashing with Node.js*).

Thankfully, Node.js already includes a function to generate random data in the `crypto` module: `randomBytes(size, callback)`.

The importance of randomness

In this book, just as in real-life applications, we're going to use random byte sequences for highly sensitive operations, such as generating encryption keys. Because of that, it's of the utmost importance to be able to have something as close as possible to true randomness. That is: given a number returned by our random number generator, an attacker should not be able to guess the next number.

Computers are deterministic machines, so, by definition, generating random numbers is a challenge for them. **True Random Number Generator** (**TRNG**) devices exist and are generally based on the observation of quantum effects; however, these are uncommon.

Instead, for most practical applications, we rely on **Cryptographically Secure Pseudo-Random Number Generators** (**CSPRNGs**), which use various sources of entropy (or "noise") to generate unpredictable numbers. These systems are generally built into the kernel of the operating systems, such as `/dev/random` on Linux, which is continuously seeded by a variety of observations that are "random" and difficult for an attacker to predict (examples include the average time between key presses on a keyboard, the timing of kernel interrupts, and others).

In Node.js, `crypto.randomBytes` returns random byte sequences using the operating system's CSPRNG, and it's considered safe for cryptographic usage.

Math.random() and Other Non-Cryptographically Safe PRNGs

Functions such as the JavaScript function `Math.random()` (which is available in Node.js too) are not cryptographically safe, and should not be used for generating random numbers or byte sequences for use in cryptographic operations.

In fact, `Math.random()` is seeded only once at the beginning of the application or script (at least this is the case of the V8 runtime as of the time of writing, in early 2021), so an attacker that managed to determine the initial seed would then be able to regenerate the same sequence of random numbers.

Within Node.js, you can verify that this is the case by invoking the `node` binary with the `--random_seed` flag to a number of your choosing and then calling `Math.random()`. You'll see that, as long as you pass the same number as the value for `--random_seed`, `Math.random()` will return the same sequence of "random" numbers even on different invocations of Node.js.

LavaRand

For an interesting discussion on TRNGs and CSPRNGs, and for a curious and fun approach to generating random entropy ("noise") to seed CSPRNGs, check out this blog post by Cloudflare explaining how they're using a wall of lava lamps in their headquarters to get safer random numbers: `https://bit.ly/crypto-lavarand`.

Using crypto.randomBytes

As mentioned, the `randomBytes(size, callback)` function from the `crypto` package is the recommended way to generate a random sequence of bytes of the length `size` that are safe for cryptographic usage.

As you can see from its signature, the function is asynchronous and it passes the result to a function that is the legacy Node.js "error-first callback" (the callback argument can be omitted, but that makes the function perform as synchronous I/O that blocks the event loop, and it's not recommended).

For example, to generate a random sequence of 32 bytes (256-bit), the traditional way of invoking the function asynchronously is as follows:

2.1: Using crypto.randomBytes

```
const crypto = require('crypto')
crypto.randomBytes(32, (err, buf) => {
```

```
    if (err) {
        throw err
    }
    console.log(buf.toString('hex'))
})
```

Executing the preceding code will print in the terminal a random, 64 character-long hex string.

As those developers who have been writing code for Node.js for longer know, the "error-first callback" style is outdated because it produced code that was harder to read, and it was prone to cause "callback hell" with many nested functions. Because of that, you'll see us in this book frequently "modernizing" these older functions, converting them to methods that return a `Promise` object and that can be used with the modern async/await pattern. To do that, we'll be using the `promisify` function from the `util` module.

For example, we can rewrite the preceding code as follows:

2.2: Using crypto.randomBytes with async/await

```
const crypto = require('crypto')
const {promisify} = require('util')
const randomBytes = promisify(crypto.randomBytes)
;(async function() {
    const buf = await randomBytes(32)
    console.log(buf.toString('hex'))
})()
```

Just like the previous code snippet, this will print a random hex string of 64 characters, but it is much more readable (especially when included in complex applications).

The `promisify` method allows us to convert functions that use the legacy "error-first callback" style into async ones (technically, functions that return `Promise` objects), so we can `await` on them.

As for `;(async function() { ... })()`, that is an asynchronous **Immediately-Invoked Function Expression (IIFE)**. It is necessary because Node.js does not allow the use of the `await` keyword outside of a function defined with the `async` modifier, so we need to define an anonymous `async` function and invoke it right away.

> **Top-Level Await**
>
> Starting with Node.js 14.8.0, support for the so-called "top-level await" (ability to use the `await` keyword at the top level, outside of a function) is available, but only in code that uses JavaScript modules, hence, with files using the `.mjs` extension. Because of that, we'll continue using the async IIFE pattern in this book.

Summary

In this chapter, we learned about two important topics that are key to using cryptographic functions. First, we learned about the most common encodings for textual strings and binary data that we'll use throughout the book, and we looked at the first code samples using the `Buffer` module in Node.js. We then explored the importance of random numbers in cryptography and learned how to generate cryptographically secure random byte sequences with Node.js.

In the next chapter, we'll start with the first class of cryptographic operations: hashing. We'll learn about how hashing differs from encryption, what it's used for, and how to hash strings, files, and stream data with Node.js. We'll also look at a few different hashing algorithms and how to pick the right one for each scenario.

Part 2 – Using Common Cryptographic Operations with Node.js

In this section, we will learn about implementing common cryptographic operations in Node.js applications, including hashing, encryption (symmetric, asymmetric, and hybrid), and digital signatures.

This section comprises the following chapters:

- *Chapter 3, File and Password Hashing with Node.js*
- *Chapter 4, Symmetric Encryption in Node.js*
- *Chapter 5, Using Asymmetric and Hybrid Encryption in Node.js*
- *Chapter 6, Digital Signatures with Node.js and Trust*

3

File and Password Hashing with Node.js

In *Chapter 1*, *Cryptography for Developers*, we introduced and listed all the cryptographic operations we'll be analyzing, including hashing, symmetric and asymmetric encryption, and digital signatures. In this chapter, we shall dive straight into the first of those: hashing.

Among the various classes of operations we'll be looking at in this book, hashing is possibly the most used one. Chances are you are already familiar with hashing at least to a degree, likely having used functions such as MD5, SHA-1, or those in the SHA-2 family previously.

Hashing's widespread and mainstream adoption in computing is a consequence of the many ways it can be used. As we'll see in this chapter, these functions help solve a wide variety of problems, including calculating checksums and verifying the integrity of documents, deriving encryption keys, storing passwords, and more.

Throughout this chapter, we'll be learning about hashing functions and their various uses, and we'll look at examples of using hashing functions with Node.js:

- First, we'll look at how hashing functions are different from ciphers, as well as their various uses.
- Using Node.js, we'll calculate SHA-2 checksums for short messages first, and then for large files, using streams.
- We'll look at how rainbow tables and other attacks can be used to "break" hashes, and why hashing functions such as SHA-2 are not appropriate for things such as password storage.
- We'll introduce password hashing and key derivation functions such as scrypt and Argon2 while providing code samples for Node.js.
- Lastly, we'll look at hashing collisions and why developers should avoid still-too-popular hashing functions such as MD5 and SHA-1.

Technical requirements

All the code samples for this chapter can be found in this book's GitHub repository at `https://bit.ly/crypto-ch3`.

An overview of hashing functions

Before we jump into the code, it's worth spending a few moments explaining what hashing functions are, how they are different from ciphers (which are functions that are used to encrypt and decrypt data), and their properties and uses.

Properties of hashing functions, and how they differ from encryption

While encryption is a two-way operation (you can encrypt a message and then decrypt it to get the original message once again), hashing is just one-way. That is, after you hash a message, you cannot retrieve the original plaintext in any way.

There are five defining characteristics of modern hashing functions:

1. As we mentioned previously, you cannot retrieve the original message from its hash (also called a digest) as hashing functions are designed as **one-way** operations.
2. Regardless of the size of the input message, the output hash has a **fixed length**. For example, SHA-256 hashes are always 32 bytes (256-bit) long, regardless of whether the input was an empty string or a blob containing multiple terabytes of data.

This means that hashing functions cause data loss by design, and that's one of the factors that contributes to making hashing functions irreversible.

3. Hashing functions are **deterministic**: given the same input message and parameters, they always return the same hash as output.

4. A small difference in input, even by just a bit, returns a completely different hash; this property is called the **avalanche effect**.

5. They're **resistant to collisions**. With modern hashing functions, it's impossible to find two messages that produce the same hash without performing a brute-force attack (we'll talk more about collisions at the end of this chapter).

The most used hashing function at this point is possibly SHA-256, which is part of the SHA-2 family. It takes any arbitrary message (as a sequence of bytes) and outputs a 32-byte (256-bit) sequence that is derived from it.

Here are some examples of SHA-256 hashes (you can generate them online using tools such as `https://bit.ly/crypto-sha2`). Note that the results are hex-encoded (as we saw in *Chapter 2, Dealing with Binary and Random Data*), so here, they're written as strings of 64 hexadecimal characters representing 32-byte binary sequences:

- `It is currently 8am` returns `c738584465e9d5ab6d3e745a6f39d05 fa7fe78fa95f5983eac658646d9599c22`.

- `It is currently 9am` returns `3a51ea05345f8e6f7f5b3eaae112c70 abb3b6f768a1387dc9c760b13dd58431f`.

    Note that the input differs from the previous one by 1 bit (the difference between the ASCII characters 8 and 9 is just 1 bit), yet the hash is completely different, as per the avalanche effect.

- An empty string (zero-length) has a SHA-256 hash too, which is `e3b0c44298fc1 c149afbf4c8996fb92427ae41e4649b934ca495991b7852b855`.

Uses for hashing functions

Developers have been using hashing functions for a variety of reasons, sometimes creatively. Here are a few examples:

- **Checking the integrity of messages or files**

    Because changes of even a single bit create completely different hashes, hashing functions are a convenient tool to check if messages or files have been accidentally corrupted or tampered with. Additionally, because hashing functions return a fixed-length string that is relatively short, the digest (also commonly referred to as a **checksum** in this context) does not add much overhead, even for very large files.

For example, when you're downloading a file from the internet, it's not uncommon to see the web page containing its checksum too, which you can use to verify that the file didn't get corrupted while in transit (or that no one maliciously made you download a different file). The following is a screenshot from the download page of Ubuntu Linux, which shows the SHA-256 digest of the ISO that is offered as a download, and it explains to users how to verify that the file you've downloaded is correct and intact:

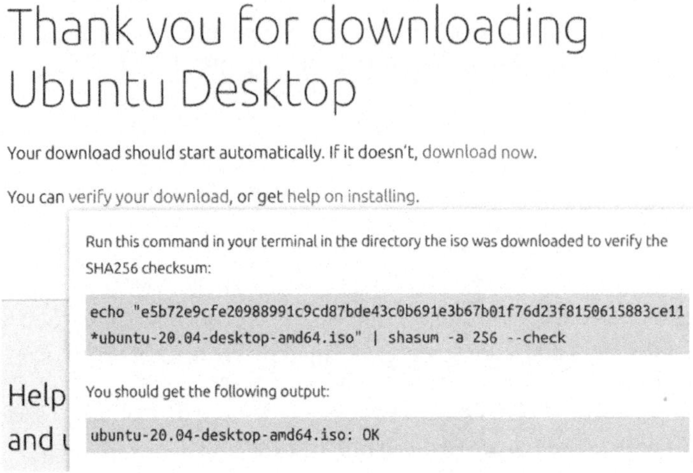

Figure 3.1 – The download page of Ubuntu Linux showing a SHA-256 checksum and instructions to verify the hash

As we'll see in *Chapter 6, Digital Signatures with Node.js and Trust*, when combining digests with asymmetric cryptography, we can get digital signatures, which offer an additional level of protection and tamper-resistance in cases like these.

- **Generating unique identifiers**

  Thanks to their collision-resistant capabilities, hashing functions can also be used to generate unique identifiers for a message, such as by hashing the message itself.

  Those who have ever used Git for source code management may be familiar with this concept: when you make a commit, Git calculates the digest from the entire set of changes and uses it as the commit's identifier.

  For example, `80ab2fddfdf30f09f0a0a637654cbb3cd5c7baa6` (on platforms such as GitHub this is often shortened to the first seven characters only, so `80ab2fd`) is the SHA-1 hash of the commit that contained the source code of MS-DOS v2.0, and it uniquely identifies that commit. If you're curious, here's the direct link to that commit on GitHub: `https://github.com/microsoft/MS-DOS/commit/80ab2fddfdf30f09f0a0a637654cbb3cd5c7baa6`.

Note that while Git tooling is currently using the outdated SHA-1 hashing function, they have begun switching to SHA-256, with experimental support added in Git 2.29 in October 2020.

- **Hashing passwords before storing them in a database**

  In a login system, hashing functions are the best way to protect users' passwords before storing them in a database. You likely already know that passwords should never be stored in a database in plaintext: hashing allows you to store them in a way that cannot be reversed (so nobody would be able to see users' passwords, even if a breach occurs). Then, because hashes are deterministic, when users are logging in, you can calculate the hash of the password they just submitted and check if it's equal to the one in the database. We'll have our first look at password hashing toward the end of this chapter.

- **Deriving encryption keys**

  We'll cover this in detail in the next chapter as we learn about symmetric ciphers. When deriving encryption keys from things such as passphrases, which can have lower entropy, using hashing functions allows us to "stretch" them, thereby offering more protection against brute-force attacks.

Hashing Functions and Blockchains

Hashing functions are a core part of blockchains such as Bitcoin and Ethereum. While every blockchain is somewhat different, at a high level, they all work by embedding the hash of the previous one in each block (hence the name blockchain); this is what enables them to have the immutability they're known for.

Computing each block in a blockchain, a process called mining, requires solving complicated problems (which, for most blockchains based on "Proof of Work", involves calculating a very large number of hashes), which takes time. Suppose you wanted to edit one block, N, in the middle of the chain (for example, to make it look like someone sent you more money than they did): this would change the hash of that block, which would then require a change in the $N+1$ block (because $N+1$ includes the hash of the N block), and then $N+2$ (as it includes the hash of $N+1$, which is now different), $N+3$, and so on. While you, a single rogue node in the network, are trying to recalculate all the blocks, each one taking a very long time, the rest of the network is continuing to mine new blocks: unless you can move faster than the rest of the network (which would require having more computing power than everyone else combined), you won't be able to get your modified block accepted by the majority of the nodes in the network. This, in a nutshell, is how hashing functions make blockchains immutable.

Now that we know about hashing functions and their properties, let's learn how to use them with Node.js.

Calculating digests and generating identifiers

Let's start by looking at how to use hashing functions with Node.js for the first two use cases presented previously – calculating the digests of messages or files to guarantee their integrity and generating unique identifiers.

For both these situations, the modern, recommended hashing function is **SHA-256**, which is part of the SHA-2 family. As its name suggests, SHA-256 returns a hash that is 256-bit in length or 32 bytes.

Other variants in the SHA-2 family exist, such as **SHA-384** or **SHA-512**, which create hashes of 384 or 512 bits (48 or 64 bytes), respectively. These, although far less common, can be useful in cases where additional resistance to collision is needed, as we'll explore at the end of this chapter.

Hashing a short message or string

With Node.js, routines to calculate SHA-256 hashes are built into the `crypto` module. Using them requires just a few lines of code, as shown in the following `sha256Digest` function:

3.1: Calculating a string's SHA-256 hash (sha2.js)

```
const crypto = require('crypto')
function sha256Digest(message, encoding) {
    return crypto.createHash('sha256')
        .update(message)
        .digest(encoding)
}

console.log(sha256Digest('Hello world!'))
console.log(sha256Digest('Hello world!', 'hex'))
console.log(sha256Digest('Hello world!', 'base64'))
```

The `crypto.createHash` method in the third line, which is part of the Node.js `crypto` module, creates a `Hash` object for using the hashing function that's passed as an argument. The full list of available hashing functions depends on the version of OpenSSL that is available on your platform, but you can safely count on finding `'sha256'`, `'sha384'`, and `'sha512'` for the SHA-2 variants mentioned previously. Legacy hashes such as `'sha1'` and `'md5'` are available too, for when your app needs compatibility with older systems; however, it's strongly recommended that you don't use them for new applications, for reasons we'll explore shortly.

After creating the `Hash` object with `createHash`, we're chaining the `update` method to add a `message` we want to hash. This function accepts both strings and `Buffer` objects, so you can pass text strings as well as binary data.

Lastly, the `digest` method calculates the hash and returns it in a `Buffer` object. Optionally, you can pass an `encoding` argument such as `'hex'`, `'base64'`, or `'base64url'` to receive the digest's encoded representation as a string instead.

If you run the previous snippet, you'll see the following output in your console, containing the SHA-256 hash of the `Hello world!` message as a `Buffer` object (when we are not passing any encoding to the `sha256Digest` function) or encoded as hex and base64 strings, respectively:

```
// sha256Digest('Hello world!')
<Buffer c0 53 5e 4b e2 b7 9f fd 93 29 13 05 43 6b f8 89 31 4e
4a 3f ae c0 5e cf fc bb 7d f3 1a d9 e5 1a>
// sha256Digest('Hello world!', 'hex')
c0535e4be2b79ffd93291305436bf889314e4a3faec05ecffcbb7df31ad9e51a
// sha256Digest('Hello world!', 'base64')
wFNeS+K3n/2TKRMFQ2v4iTFOSj+uwF7P/Lt98xrZ5Ro=
```

Hashing large files and streams

The conciseness of the `sha256Digest` function defined in *Sample 2.1* makes it fairly straightforward to implement in any application and it's perfect for hashing relatively short strings or messages. However, it also requires the entire plaintext data to be passed in the `message` argument, which means that your message has to be fully loaded in memory beforehand. When you're dealing with large files or streams of data of an unknown length (for example, documents that are received over the network) that might not be desirable, if not outright impossible.

Thankfully for us, each `Hash` object (as created by `crypto.createHash`) natively support Node.js streams, so you can pipe your message directly into it, as shown in the following `sha256DigestStream` method:

3.2: Calculating the hash of a stream (sha2-stream.js)

```
const crypto = require('crypto')
function sha256DigestStream(read, encoding) {
    return new Promise((resolve, reject) => {
        const hash = crypto.createHash('sha256')
        read.on('error', (err) => {
            reject(err)
        })
        read.on('end', () => {
            resolve(hash.digest(encoding))
        })
        read.pipe(hash)
    })
}
```

In typical Node.js fashion, as soon as we introduce streams, the code suddenly becomes far more complex, so let's look at it section by section.

To start, the signature of the `sha256DigestStream` function is very similar to the one of `sha256Digest` that we saw in the previous example, but rather than taking the full message (as a string or `Buffer`) as the first argument, this one accepts a readable stream in the `read` parameter: `sha256DigestStream(read, encoding)` (we'll see an example of creating a readable stream from a file in a moment).

Because streams are asynchronous by nature, inside the function, we immediately create and return a `Promise` object. By doing this, we make our function asynchronous, so we can invoke it with the `await` keyword, as we'll see in its sample usage shortly.

Promises in JavaScript

In JavaScript, promises were introduced with ES2015 (ES6) as a way to return a value that is not immediately available. When you create a `Promise` object, you pass a function to the constructor that accepts two parameters called `resolve` and `reject`, both of which are callbacks as well. You can perform asynchronous code inside the function (for example, making network requests or, in our case, parsing a stream of data) and when you're done, you can invoke the `resolve` callback with the value to return; in case of an error, you can invoke `reject` instead.

In functions that have been created with the `async` modifier, you can use the `await` keyword on a `Promise` object to pause the execution until the promise is resolved (fulfilled or rejected).

For a well-written primer on promises, go to `https://bit.ly/crypto-promises`.

Inside the promise's callback, we create a `Hash` object with `crypto.createHash`, just like in the previous example. However, rather than passing the entire message to its `update` method, we use `read.pipe(hash)` to pipe from the `read` input stream into the `hash` object (which can be used as a writable stream).

Finally, we are attaching two callbacks to the `read` input stream:

- When the input stream ends (that is, when all the data has been read, such as when we reach the end of the file), we invoke the `resolve` method of the promise and pass the hash's digest as the returned value. If we passed an `encoding` parameter to `sha256DigestStream`, then that is passed to `hash.digest` too, as in the previous example:

```
read.on('end', () => {
    resolve(hash.digest(encoding))
})
```

- We also listen for errors, such as if the input stream abruptly ends (for example, if you're reading from a network and the connection drops). In that case, we invoke the promise's `reject` method with the error as an argument:

```
read.on('error', (err) => {
    reject(err)
})
```

While the implementation of `sha256DigestStream` is a bit more complex, it can be conveniently used as an async function; for example:

3.3: Using sha256DigestStream

```
const fs = require('fs')
async function hashFile(path) {
    const read = fs.createReadStream(path)
    const digest = await sha256DigestStream(read, 'hex')
    console.log(digest)
}
hashFile('photo.jpg')
```

In this example, we're creating an async function called `hashFile` that starts by creating a readable stream in a file (`fs.createReadStream(path)` using the Node.js `fs` module for operations on the local filesystem) and then passes it to our `sha256DigestStream` method. Because `sha256DigestStream` returns a `Promise`, we can use it as an async function, so we can `await` on it.

Running the preceding function will show the SHA-256 digest of the file in the console (in the preceding example, of a file named `photo.jpg`), and this will work with files of every size, even those that are multiple gigabytes! Try it with a large file on your laptop.

At the beginning of this section, we mentioned that hashing functions such as those in the SHA-2 family are excellent for calculating digests of messages (to guarantee their integrity) or for generating unique identifiers as Git does. However, we also said that these functions should not be leveraged for some other, more sensitive uses, such as hashing passwords or deriving encryption keys. To understand why, we need to look at how hashes can be "broken."

How to "break" a hash

Let me start by offering an apology for perhaps misnaming this section. In *Chapter 1, Cryptography for Developers*, we explained that "breaking" a cryptographic algorithm requires finding ways to derive the plaintext – or, in the case of hashes, finding collisions – without performing brute-force attacks (more on collisions at the end of this chapter).

So far, as I'm writing this book, SHA-2 hashes have not been "broken." This means that no one has found vulnerabilities that make them significantly less secure, which happened to older (but still very popular) hashing functions such as MD5 and SHA-1, for which practical collision attacks have been demonstrated.

Yet, it's still not recommended to use SHA-2 on low-entropy inputs, such as passwords. The problem, which may come as a surprise to some, is that SHA-2 is too *fast* to compute.

Fast hashing functions and low-entropy inputs

When you store passwords or derive encryption keys, using a fast hashing function is, unintuitively, a bad thing as it lowers the difficulty of performing a brute-force attack.

Suppose an attacker managed to break into your database and found that the SHA-256 hash of the admin password is `2cf24dba5fb0a30e26e83b2ac5b9e29e1b161e5c1 fa7425e73043362938b9824`. Because SHA-256 hasn't been "broken" yet, the only way an attacker would be able to find the original password that corresponds to that hash is via a brute-force attack.

SHA-256 hashes are 256-bit in length, which means that there are 2^{256} possible combinations, or about 10^{77}. This is an insanely huge number, and an attacker who wanted to try computing each hash would need many billions of years, even with the fastest supercomputers available today (far longer than the expected lifespan of the universe).

However, passwords aren't perfectly random strings, and they are considered low-entropy inputs.

In information theory, **entropy** is, at a very high level, a measure of how much information is needed to represent a random event. More surprising events (that is, less likely) require more information to represent them, so they have higher entropy. Glossing over the formal definition of entropy or the details of how to calculate it (in this case, *the base two logarithm of the total number of possible combinations for that event*), we shall limit ourselves to saying that the more complex the password, the higher its entropy measured in bits. Let's look at some examples:

- A typical 4-digit padlock, each with numbers 0 to 9, has a total of 10,000 combinations. Assuming that a user picked a completely, truly random combination, they would have about 13.3 bits of entropy (`log2(10000)`).

- A random, 8-character password that used only lowercase letters (there are 26 letters in the Latin alphabet) would have a total of 26^8 combinations, so its entropy (assuming the password is truly random) would be about 37.6 bits (`log2(26^8)`).

- An ideal 256-bit encryption key is a key file with 32 random bytes (that is 256-bit). In this case, there are 2^{256} different combinations, so there are 256 bits of entropy.

It's important to note that entropy is logarithmic, so if the number of bits of entropy doubles (for example, from 10 to 20), the number of possible combinations is elevated to the power of two (from 2^{10} to 2^{20}), so the effort that's required to brute-force that password is squared (with the effort being the product of time and computing power).

Going back to our admin password's hash (`2cf24dba5fb0a30e26e83b2ac5b9e29e 1b161e5c1fa7425e73043362938b9824`), an attacker doesn't need to calculate every possible random byte sequence (2^{256} or about 10^{77}) – they just need to find common sequences of characters. The attacker could start by calculating the hash of all the words in the English dictionary (just over 170,000, which is a ridiculously small number of combinations for a brute-force attack), and they would quickly find that our admin password is `hello` since its SHA-256 matches the one shown previously.

As we mentioned previously, the core issue is that SHA-2 hashes can be calculated too fast, also leveraging hardware-accelerated solutions. Attackers can compute a lot of SHA-2 hashes per second using GPUs (video cards), FPGAs, or even dedicated ASIC chips. Incidentally, the demand for more efficient hardware to mine Bitcoins (which is based on SHA hashes) has made hardware solutions for calculating SHA hashes fast, efficient, easy to find, and cheap, and those can be repurposed for brute-forcing password hashes too.

Consumer-grade GPUs in 2021 can calculate tens of millions of SHA hashes per second, so they could crack the hash of every English word in less than 1 second. At the time of writing, the world's most powerful calculator of SHA hashes, which is the network of all Bitcoin miners, is estimated to be able to calculate 180 exa-hashes per second, or a staggering $1.8 * 10^{20}$ hashes every second (growing from 100 exa-hashes per second just 1 year prior). Security experts have been worried for a while that, during times when cryptocurrency prices are low and so mining may not be cost-effective, people with access to large mining rigs could make profits by switching to cracking password hashes instead.

Rainbow tables

If what I wrote in the previous section wasn't enough to scare you, one other major issue with regular SHA-2 hashes is that they can be subject to rainbow table attacks, making them even less desirable for hashing passwords.

A **rainbow table** is a dataset of pre-computed hashes (for example, SHA-256 hashes) stored together with their corresponding plaintext string. For example, these datasets would store both a message (`SUPER_safe_passw0rd!`) and its corresponding hash (`ad5d09462eafb41f110dae8fecd1f7de98f7c3056edd033c56fb8949720 fedb2`), so "reversing" the hash would be as simple as performing a lookup in the dataset.

Around the world, attackers have pre-computed large datasets with all the words contained in a dictionary, all the passwords with letters and numbers shorter than N characters, and so on. Attackers also harvest data from password breaches that contain plaintext passwords and include those too, as they're guaranteed to be passwords that are used by at least one person. By pre-computing all the hashes for what common (or likely) passwords are, cracking a hash can be instantaneous.

Some websites (even in the "non-dark" web) offer the ability to look up hashes in their rainbow tables for free. For example, one of them, which we won't name here but that you can find very easily, claims to include a rainbow table with 1.5 billion SHA-2 hashes.

Using a **salt** when hashing passwords is a quick solution to stop generic rainbow tables from working. This means adding a prefix (or suffix) to every single password before hashing it (for example, adding "foobar" before passwords, so each password is hashed as `sha256('foobar'+password)`).

However, salts are not secret by definition, since they're stored in the application's source code or the database next to the password. So, an attacker who managed to get ahold of the salt could generate a new rainbow table for all the common passwords using that salt relatively quickly.

Even if each salt were used only once, meaning that you generate a new, random one for each password, SHA-2 hashes can be calculated so fast for passwords that the security that's offered by salted SHA-2 is still considered not adequate (*but if you really must use SHA-2, salting the passwords is certainly better than not doing it*).

The bottom line is that even though SHA-2 hashes are not technically "broken," they are not adequate for protecting passwords or deriving keys from low-entropy inputs. Even when you're using salts, they can be brute-forced too quickly. So, for those uses, we need to look at other hashing functions, which are slower by design.

Hashing passwords and deriving keys

As we saw in the previous section, passwords have a low entropy, so when you need to hash them so that they can be stored in a database or when you want to derive encryption keys from them, you should be using deliberately slow hashing functions.

In a world where computers continue to get faster and developers strive to create applications that run in less time and use fewer resources, the existence of an entire field of research around creating purposely slow algorithms may feel odd. Yet, in the field of hashing functions, there's a whole class of algorithms (sometimes called **Key Derivation Functions (KDFs)** in this case) that are designed to do just that.

Among all the various KDFs, we will be looking specifically at two: **Argon2** and **scrypt**. These are designed to be slow, with a configurable "cost" for each invocation, and they aim to make it harder to use hardware accelerators such as GPUs or FPGAs.

The Case for Leveraging Identity-as-a-Service

In this section, we're covering how to hash passwords, which is commonly done by developers while implementing authentication within an application. However, we'd be doing you a disservice if we didn't mention that rolling your authentication and user management is not only unnecessary nowadays, but outright discouraged in many (most?) cases. Instead, we recommend leveraging external identity providers such as Identity-as-a-Service solutions (for example, Auth0, Azure AD, Google Identity Platform, Okta, and so on) for both internal "line of business" applications and external-facing ones. Besides allowing developers to focus their time on other parts of the solution that provide more business value than authentication, they offer benefits to end users too, such as the ability to use a single account, a familiar flow, and more. Additionally, thanks to their size, these identity providers can offer levels of security far beyond what in-house solutions can. To learn more, please go to `https://bit.ly/crypto-auth`.

Argon2

Argon2 should be your default choice when available. It's a relatively new algorithm, but it won the Password Hashing Competition in 2015.

It is available in two variants, **Argon2i** and **Argon2d**, both of which are hardened against two specific kinds of attacks (side-channels and GPU-cracking, respectively). There's also a third, hybrid variant called **Argon2id**, which mixes both, and according to the official specifications, it's the best one to use unless you have a reason to pick one of the others.

One interesting aspect of Argon2 is that it tries not only to be deliberately slow (with a time cost that is configurable by the developer) but it's specifically designed to require a larger amount of memory and make it harder to compute with GPUs and other hardware.

With Node.js, Argon2 is available in the `argon2` package from NPM (`https://www.npmjs.com/package/argon2`), which, under the hood, is a wrapper around the reference implementation and is considered safe.

Because it's not available inside the Node.js runtime, to use Argon2, you need to install it from NPM with this command:

```
npm install argon2
```

To calculate a hash using Argon2, you can invoke the `argon2.hash` method, like so:

```
const argon2 = require('argon2')
;(async function() {
    const passphrase = 'correct horse battery staple'
    const hash = await argon2.hash(passphrase, {
        type: argon2.argon2id,
    })
    console.log('Hash is:', hash)
})()
```

To start, note that we're wrapping the code inside an async **Immediately-Invoked Function Expression (IIFE)** because we cannot use the `await` keyword outside of a function defined with the `async` keyword.

As you can see, the `argon2.hash` method requires two parameters – the password/passphrase to hash and an options dictionary. The latter is a plain object that can be used to configure the behaviour of the key derivation function, including the type of hash (here, you can see we're setting `type: argon2.argon2id` to tell the method to use the Argon2id variant), the cost, and the memory requirements.

You can see the full list of options that can be passed to `argon2.hash` in the official documentation at `https://bit.ly/crypto-argon2-options`. For most users, aside from setting the type to Argon2id, using the defaults should be a reasonable choice to get started.

"correct horse battery staple"

The curious passphrase that we used in the preceding example first appeared in Randall Munroe's popular XKCD vignette (post #936). Not only does the vignette itself do an excellent job of explaining password security, but its page on the "Explain XKCD" wiki contains a lot of information on password cracking, entropy, and other relevant topics, and it's well worth a read: `https://bit.ly/crypto-xkcd-936`.

The value of the `hash` variable is a string and, if your goal is to hash a password, it's safe to store that in the database.

Interestingly, if you run the preceding code, you will see that the output is a different hash every time and that it looks quite different from the hashes we generated earlier in this chapter. For example, during one execution, we got the following output:

```
Hash is: $argon2id$v=19$m=4096,t=3,p=1$hKNpdd8v7A4eRByhWQ/
HTA$FD6+Wsl1276ROPJvzJT0+hmIFKiBvMRk39ILu2H/b9k
```

As you can see, the beginning of the hash contains a list of all the options that were used to generate the hash (the Argon2 variant, the version, and the parameters for memory, time, and parallelism). The hash is base64-encoded and begins after the last $ sign.

At the beginning of this chapter, we mentioned that hashing functions are deterministic, so given an input message, they return the same hash every time. Yet, the result of `argon2.hash` is different on every invocation. The reason for this is that the method internally generates a random salt for every new hash, and it prepends that to the hash – in the preceding string, the highlighted hKNpdd8v7A4 is the random salt (base64-encoded), and the actual hash follows.

The fact that `argon2.hash` has many user-configurable options is the reason why all these values and the salt have to be prepended to the hash. If you are using `argon2.hash` to hash a password before storing it in a database, you will need to store that additional information to be able to re-compute the same hash later, deterministically, and check if the password that's been supplied by the user during a login attempt matches the one in the database.

Fortunately, this entire process is simpler than it sounds as the same package includes the `argon2.verify(hash, passphrase)` method, which does all the necessary calculations for us. You just need to invoke it (asynchronously) by passing the hash that you stored in your database and the password that was submitted by the user; the method returns `true` if the passwords match. For example:

```
if (await argon2.verify(hash, passphrase)) {
    console.log('Passphrases match')
}
else {
    console.log('Passphrases don't match')
}
```

Note that this method is asynchronous too, so to invoke it with the `await` keyword, it must be used inside a function defined with the `async` modifier.

Scrypt

Alternatively, you can use **scrypt** as a key derivation function. While Argon2 is possibly a better option for its resistance to side-channel attacks and hardware/GPU cracking, scrypt has been around for longer, which means it has broader support across programming languages and frameworks.

With Node.js, scrypt is available in the standard library, so you don't need to import an external package from NPM to use it; for example:

3.4: Generating a hash with scrypt (scrypt-generate.js)

```js
const crypto = require('crypto')
const {promisify} = require('util')

const scrypt = promisify(crypto.scrypt)
const randomBytes = promisify(crypto.randomBytes)

async function scryptHash(passphrase) {
    const saltLength = 16
    const salt = await randomBytes(saltLength)
    const hash = await scrypt(passphrase, salt, 32)

    // console.log statements for debug purposes only
    console.log('Hash:', hash.toString('hex'))
    console.log('Salt:', salt.toString('hex'))

    const stored = Buffer.concat(
        [salt, hash]
    ).toString('base64')

    return stored
}

;(async function() {
    const passphrase = 'correct horse battery staple'
    const stored = await scryptHash(passphrase)
    console.log('Store value:', stored)
})()
```

Conceptually, this is very similar to the Argon2 generation example, but the scrypt module requires us to do a bit more work in our code.

To start, we have defined an asynchronous scryptHash(passphrase) function that returns the hash for the passphrase parameter that was calculated using scrypt. Then, just as we did previously, we have an async IIFE in which we invoke await scryptHash to get the result.

Outside of the functions, in the beginning, we are importing the crypto package (which includes the scrypt and randomBytes methods). These methods in the crypto package return their asynchronous results using the older *error-first callback* pattern. To modernize them and be able to invoke the methods with await, we are using the promisify method from the util package (in the third and fourth lines of code).

Inside the scryptHash function, we need to generate a 16-byte random salt (unlike with the argon2 module from NPM we used, we are responsible for doing that ourselves in this case). With Node.js, we can use the crypto.randomBytes method, which we promisified in the preceding code to be able to invoke it with await randomBytes(saltLength).

We then use the (promisified) crypto.scrypt(passphrase, salt, length) method to generate a new scrypt hash. We are requesting 32 bytes in length to get a 256-bit hash.

Both the randomBytes and scrypt methods return Buffer objects.

Lastly, to know what value to store in the database, we are computing the stored variable, which is a Buffer that contains the concatenation of the random salt and the computed hash. We are immediately calculating the base64 representation of stored, which is a string that we can store in our database.

Running the preceding code will print something like the following in the console (because the salt is randomly generated every time, the values will be different on every invocation):

```
Hash: fef57139fd36d497d95c4f9918c460bed7bccfb77fca1ba2b32f91793
ee3bdaa
```
```
Salt: b0424b429936053974412a1a8b55f184
```
```
Store value: sEJLQpk2BT10QSoai1XxhP71cTn9NtSX2VxPmRjEYL7XvM+3f8
oborMvkXk+472q
```

When a user logs in again, you will need to verify the hash by following this process:

1. Retrieve the value of stored from your database, then decode it from base64 (using Buffer.from(stored, 'base64')).

2. Extract the first 16 bytes from the decoded value to use as a salt (the rest will be the hash). To do this, we can use the `Buffer.slice(start, length)` method twice: first to get the first 16 bytes (`start=0` and `length=16`), and then to get all the rest until the end (`start=16` and no length).

3. Invoke `crypto.scrypt(checkPassphrase, salt, length)` again with the salt extracted from the preceding step, but using the password submitted by the user; use the same length you did previously (`32`).

4. Check if the result of the function in *Step 3* matches the hash that was extracted in *Step 2*: if they are the same, then the password that was submitted by the user is correct. Because both objects to compare are buffers, we need to use the `Buffer.compare(a, b)` method, which returns `0` if they are equal.

We can implement the preceding algorithm in the `scryptVerify` function like so:

3.5: Verifying a hash with scrypt (scrypt-verify.js)

```
const crypto = require('crypto')
const scrypt = require('util').promisify(crypto.scrypt)
async function scryptVerify(stored, passphrase) {
    const saltLength = 16
    const buf = Buffer.from(stored, 'base64')
    const salt = buf.slice(0, saltLength)
    const hash = buf.slice(saltLength)
    const verifyHash = await scrypt(passphrase, salt, 32)
    return verifyHash.compare(hash) === 0
}


;(async function() {
    const passphrase = '<passphrase from the user>'
    const stored = '<base64-encoded value retrieved from the
        database>'
    if (await scryptVerify(stored, passphrase)) {
        console.log('Passphrases match')
    }
    else {
        console.log('Passphrases don\'t match')
    }
})()
```

Invoking `await scryptVerify` returns true if the passphrase that's sent by the user during a login attempt matches the hash that was stored in the database.

> **Parameters for scrypt**
>
> The `crypto.scrypt` function supports an additional `options` parameter, which is an object that allows us to control how many resources the hashing function will use. A full reference of all the options and their default values can be found in the official documentation at `https://bit.ly/crypto-scrypt`.
>
> Please note that unlike with Argon2, the result of the scrypt invocation in Node.js never contains the full list of parameters that were used to compute the hash, so it's your responsibility to document them clearly for when you need to re-compute the same hash (such as when you want to match a user's password during sign in).

With this section, we have completed our overview of the hashing and key derivation functions that we should be using, for both calculating checksums and for hashing passwords and deriving keys: SHA-2, Argon2, and scrypt.

We mentioned that there are many more hashing functions, including some older ones that should be avoided. Given how popular some of those are, it's worth taking a look at why.

Older hashing functions

We began this book by promising that we wouldn't be covering older cryptographic functions, so it seems appropriate to break that promise as early as in the third chapter.

The reason why we are not apologizing for our "misdeed" is that there are lots of hashing functions that are broken and yet are still too widely used and talked about, so it is worth taking a quick look at what's wrong with them and why they should be avoided.

Among the hashing functions that you should **not use**, we need to highlight the following:

- **MD5** and **SHA-1** are considered precursors to SHA-2. Researchers have found vulnerabilities in them that allow attackers to generate collisions in minutes (more on that shortly), so these algorithms are considered effectively broken.

- **PBKDF2** is an older key derivation function that was used for password hashing too. While not broken, it's not recommended to be used as a key derivation function anymore.

At a high level, PBKDF2 works by executing multiple iterations of SHA-2 (sometimes thousands) over the original message to slow down attackers. However, because it's based on SHA-2, which is very fast to compute with GPUs and specialized hardware, nowadays it succeeds at slowing down attackers only marginally, and it's not as effective anymore.

- **bcrypt** is also an older password hashing and key derivation function, and while it's a better choice than PBKDF2, it's still potentially more vulnerable to cracking with GPUs or dedicated chips. While bcrypt is not *bad*, Argon2 and scrypt are arguably superior choices at this time.

Collisions

We mentioned the problem of collisions very briefly at the beginning of this chapter, but it's now time to look at it a bit more in detail.

As we wrote many times, a SHA-256 hash is 256 bits long, so there are a total of 2^{256} possible hashes that can be generated. While that is a… ginormous number, it's still a finite one. Given a certain message, then, there will always be other messages that have the same SHA-256 digest.

The situation where two different messages have the same digest is known as a **collision**.

These collisions happening is an inevitable fact; however, with the space of all possible hashes being so vast, the probability of that happening with two random messages is essentially zero. For example, after calculating 1 billion random SHA-256 hashes, the probability of a collision is approximately in the order of magnitude of 1 in 10^{60} (to put that in perspective, the probability of getting hit by a meteorite is estimated to be around 1 in 10^6).

Nevertheless, the SHA-2 family offers longer variants too, namely SHA-384 and SHA-512 (of 384 and 512 bits, respectively) for when a longer hash is desired.

So far, we've talked about collisions as random, extremely unlikely, events. As we mentioned at the beginning of this chapter, modern hashing functions are ideally collision-resistant, which means that given a certain message and its digest, the only way to find another message with the same digest would be to perform a brute-force attack.

However, researchers trying to break hashing functions over the decades have particularly focused on finding ways to generate collisions in a significantly shorter time, sometimes instantaneously.

In the case of hashing functions such as MD5 and SHA-1, researchers have been able to demonstrate practical ways to perform **collision attacks**: they have been able to create algorithms to generate multiple messages with the same hash in practical amounts of time. As a consequence, MD5 and SHA-1 are now considered broken and should be avoided.

Collision attacks have real, practical implications. For example, hashes are used with certificates – such as TLS certificates – to identify them (this is another example of using hashes to generate unique identifiers, just like Git does): when attackers can generate collisions, they may be able to make clients accept a different certificate than they were expecting (we'll talk about certificates in more detail in *Chapter 6, Digital Signatures with Node.js and Trust*). A similar scenario was demonstrated in practice with MD5, prompting an acceleration of the need to deprecate TLS certificates with MD5 hashes (at the time of writing, all browsers require TLS certificates to use SHA-2 only).

Summary

In this chapter, we covered hashing, the first of the cryptographic operations we will be exploring in this book. Hashing functions can be used by developers for a variety of purposes: in particular, we've looked at SHA-2 as the recommended function for calculating digests of files and messages (to verify their integrity or to generate identifiers), and Argon2 and scrypt for storing passwords and deriving encryption keys. We've also looked at the issues that impact hashing functions, and why older algorithms are to be avoided.

In the next chapter, we're going to cover encryption and decryption using symmetric ciphers, the first of the two kinds we'll be studying in this book, using two popular algorithms – AES and ChaCha20-Poly1305. We'll also put what we saw in this chapter into practice and use hashing functions to derive symmetric encryption keys safely.

4

Symmetric Encryption in Node.js

If you stopped a random person on the street and asked them what is the first thing that comes to their mind when they think of cryptography, chances are they'd talk about encrypting their data and protecting it with a password or PIN. This class of operations is called symmetric encryption, and it's arguably the most widely known, even among not particularly tech-savvy consumers.

In *Chapter 3, File and Password Hashing with Node.js*, we began looking at classes of cryptographic operations. starting with hashing functions, and we explained how they're different from encryption. While hashing is a one-way operation, encryption is reversible: you can obtain the plaintext back from an encrypted message (also called **ciphertext**).

In this chapter, we'll look at data encryption using symmetric algorithms, specifically AES and ChaCha20-Poly1305, by covering the following topics:

- The difference between symmetric and asymmetric ciphers

- Symmetric encryption and decryption with AES, with code samples for Node.js

- Using ChaCha20-Poly1305 with Node.js

- How to derive symmetric encryption keys from passphrases
- How (and why) to wrap symmetric keys with AES-KW using Node.js

Technical requirements

All the code samples for this chapter can be found in this book's GitHub repository at `https://bit.ly/crypto-ch4`.

Symmetric and asymmetric encryption

There are two main kinds of ciphers (and, consequentially, of encryption): symmetric and asymmetric, and the difference lies in the kind of keys that are used.

Symmetric encryption is probably the most well-known of the two, and the one that consumers are more likely to be familiar with as well. With symmetric encryption, you encrypt data using a key, and then use the very same key to decrypt it again. In many cases, the key can be derived from a password or passphrase, as we'll see at the end of this chapter.

Conceptually, algorithms such as AES (one of the most popular and widely used symmetric ciphers) and ChaCha20-Poly1305 work this way.

If you wanted to share the encrypted message with another person, you'd need to provide the other party with both the ciphertext (the encrypted data) and the key. Like many people, even consumers have experienced, in this case, the challenge of sharing the encryption key securely. Having the ciphertext and the key is both necessary and sufficient to decrypt the data, which means that great care must be put into protecting symmetric keys (in cryptography, it's assumed that the ciphertext doesn't necessarily need to be kept a secret). This can be especially problematic when you are transferring data over an untrusted channel, such as the Internet.

For example, consider a scenario in which you need to email a friend an encrypted ZIP file. If you send the key/passphrase together with the encrypted data (for example, you write the passphrase in the body of the email and add the ciphertext as an attachment), an attacker that's eavesdropping could steal both at the same time, voiding the protection offered by encryption.

To solve these issues, we can use **asymmetric encryption**. With that, there are two different, but related, keys: a private one and a public one.

With asymmetric encryption, you encrypt data with a public key and decrypt it with the corresponding private key.

This makes sharing data over an untrusted channel easier: if your friend wanted to send you an encrypted message, they'd only need the public part of your key to encrypt it. They'd then send the ciphertext to you, and you'd use your private key to decrypt it. The public key alone is not sufficient (nor necessary) to decrypt a ciphertext, and once your friend has encrypted what they wanted to send you, it can only be decrypted with your private key.

There are various algorithms for asymmetric encryption, sometimes called public-key cryptography, with RSA being one of the most popular ones.

Public key (asymmetric) cryptography is more complex than the symmetric one, both conceptually and in how it's used in practice. Going back to the previous example in which you were trying to send a ZIP file to a friend protected with encryption, you could safely do so with S/MIME or GPG, two standards and sets of tools that leverage public key cryptography to remove the issue of having to share the symmetric key. Both those standards have been around for a while, tracing their roots back to the 1990s. Yet, if you've never heard of them before, or if you're very confused by how they are set up and used, you are in very good company: the complexity of using them and the limited support in apps such as email clients makes their adoption fairly small, especially among the general public.

Even though asymmetric encryption may lack in how it's understood and leveraged *with intention* by the general public, it's still widely used, daily and transparently, by virtually every person on Earth. For example, public-key cryptography is what makes protocols such as TLS and HTTPS, which are foundational to the modern Internet, possible – among many other things that underpin common everyday activities.

Now that you understand the two different kinds of ciphers, we're going to dedicate this chapter to symmetric ones, starting with AES. We'll cover asymmetric ciphers in more detail in *Chapter 5, Using Asymmetric and Hybrid Encryption in Node.js*, and *Chapter 6, Digital Signatures with Node.js and Trust*, where we will cover data encryption and digital signatures, respectively.

Symmetric encryption with AES

The **Advanced Encryption Standard** (**AES**) is one of the most widely used symmetric ciphers, and it's been like that since its standardization in the early 2000s. It's safe (approved by the US government for encrypting "top secret" documents) and fast, with support available in all operating systems and programming languages.

Additionally, hardware acceleration for AES is available in all modern desktop and server CPUs (for example, the AES-NI instructions in Intel and AMD processors), as well as in a large number of mobile/embedded chips, making executing AES rather cheap in terms of computing power. A regular consumer-grade CPU can easily encrypt or decrypt AES streams at the speed of multiple gigabits per second. Many consumer operating systems are now encrypting hard drives by default, transparently to the user, using AES – that's the case of BitLocker on Windows and FileVault on macOS, for example.

To use AES, you need a key that is 128-, 192-, or 256-bit in length, and these keys should either be random sequences of bytes or derived from a passphrase using a Key Derivation Function (we'll look at how to derive a key from a passphrase at the end of this chapter).

Before we dive into using AES with code samples, however, we need to look at three important aspects, including two decisions we need to make (the length of the encryption key and the mode of operation) and the concept of initialization vectors.

Key length

The first thing we should discuss is the length of the key. We mentioned that the standard for AES defines three different key lengths: **128, 192, or 256 bits** (16, 24, or 32 bytes, respectively), with 192-bit keys rarely used in practice. Shorter keys are not allowed in the standard, and even if they were, you'd be strongly advised against using them.

As we saw in *Chapter 1*, *Cryptography for Developers*, algorithms that haven't been broken – and AES has certainly not been broken yet – can only be cracked using brute force. This means an attacker would have to try every single combination that is possible and hope to find the right one. Although brute-force attacks are always possible in theory, the goal of the defending party is to make them impossible in practice, by making the effort required by an attacker (time and energy) too big to even attempt.

When deciding between the various sizes, you might think that 256-bit is safer, and you'd be correct *in theory*. By using twice as many bits for the key's length, a successful brute-force attack against AES-256 would require something significantly more effort: not *double*, but the *square* (power of two) of the time.

In practice, using a 128-bit key is generally safe at the time of writing and for the foreseeable future. As we saw in the *Defining safe* section of *Chapter 1, Cryptography for Developers*, even leveraging the entire computing power of every Bitcoin miner (which aren't optimized for brute-forcing AES, but we hypothetically assume they could be repurposed for that), it would take 10^{10} years to break AES with a 128-bit key, which is comparable with the age of the Universe. This means that even though AES-256 does provide significantly more strength than AES-128 in theory, *in practical terms*, the protection they offer can safely be considered equal. At the same time, AES-128 is faster due to performing fewer rounds of the algorithm (10 rounds instead of 14).

Yet, this is not the end of the argument.

After convincing you that AES-128 offers essentially the same security as AES-256 in practical terms, it's worth pointing out that unless your application is particularly sensitive to the performance loss, you may want to adopt 256-bit keys for AES regardless.

When 1Password (a popular password manager app) migrated from using 128-bit to 256-bit keys for AES, their "Chief Defender Against the Dark Arts" Jeffrey Goldberg wrote a well-thought and well-explained piece on that (`https://bit.ly/crypto-aes256`). The reasons for that choice can be applied to a lot of other applications too, and we can summarize them in three points:

- AES-256 provides double the key size but is only 40% slower than AES-128 (14 rounds instead of 10), rather than twice as slow. On modern systems, AES is really fast, especially when hardware acceleration is available, so the extra performance cost of using 256-bit keys is negligible for most applications.

- As we mentioned in *Chapter 1, Cryptography for Developers*, quantum computing can pose a threat to certain cryptographic algorithms, and AES is one of them. Against a quantum computer, AES key sizes are effectively halved, so a 128-bit key has the strength of a 64-bit one (which means that the time needed for a brute force is its square root).

  At the time of writing, this is a purely theoretical threat: we're still far from quantum computers that could be used to mount practical attacks against AES keys even smaller than 64-bit. Virtually all quantum computers in existence today are experimental ones in advanced research labs, and it's unclear how long it will take before they will be able to break a 64-bit key in a practical amount of time.

- Lastly, there are psychological and marketing aspects involved. 256-bit keys sound better than 128-bit ones, so it can make people feel more comfortable to use the longer keys, even if, in practice, they're equally safe.

To summarize, in practice **both 128-bit and 256-bit keys are equally safe**.

If you need your code to run as fast as possible or are processing very large amounts of data, it's perfectly fine to use a 128-bit key.

However, if your system can tolerate the slightly longer processing required by a 256-bit key, you may want to use them to protect against the possible future threats of quantum computing, and because of the psychological effects.

Mode of operation

The other decision we need to make is the mode of operation. AES can be used with a variety of modes of operation; looking at each is beyond the scope of this book.

We can limit ourselves to two that we can recommend for most applications:

- **AES-CBC** (Cipher Block Chaining) when you don't need authentication
- **AES-GCM** (Galois/Counter Mode) when you need authentication

We will mostly ignore the other modes of operation in this book. There are situations where they can be useful, but those are much less common and are specific to certain applications or domains.

Something worth mentioning, given how often it's mentioned in articles online, is that it's very important **not** to use the **AES-ECB** mode (Electronic Code Book). This is the simplest of all modes, but it is not suitable for encrypting data larger than one block (16 to 32 bytes, depending on the size of the key) because each block of the message is encrypted independently. The result does not hide the plaintext well, as you can see with your own eyes:

Figure 4.1 – Encrypting an image (the Packt logo at the top) with AES-ECB (middle) and other AES modes (bottom)

Here, the original image at the top is encrypted with AES-EBC in the middle. Even though it's encrypted, it's possible to see the original image's "shape." Using AES in any other mode returns an image like the one at the bottom, which looks "random."

Going back to our two recommended modes of operation, the next thing we need to cover is authenticated encryption. All modes of operation ensure confidentiality, meaning that if you encrypt a message, no one should be able to understand it from the ciphertext.

Authenticated Encryption (**AE**) means that not only is the data encrypted (guaranteeing confidentiality), but also that a "tag" is added to guarantee the integrity of the message when it's decrypted. This is useful if you want to ensure that it's possible to determine whether anyone has altered the ciphertext. The tag works similarly to a hash/checksum, but it's calculated efficiently while the data is being encrypted.

When using AE, if someone were to alter the ciphertext, when you decrypt it, the authentication check would fail. Without AE, while the attacker would still be unable to decrypt your ciphertext, they could alter it and make you decrypt invalid data: this may corrupt your application's state or cause other unintended consequences.

> **Authenticated ciphers and decrypting data**
>
> Note that because the integrity of the message cannot be verified until the ciphertext has been decrypted in full, your application should not begin processing data until the decryption process is complete and the authentication tag has been validated. This means, for example, that if you're decrypting a stream that was encrypted with an authenticated cipher, you first need to decrypt it entirely and verify the authentication tag before you can begin processing it; otherwise, there's no guarantee that the data you're working with hadn't been tampered with.
>
> In some cases, when fully decrypting a stream is not possible or not desirable, an option is to chunk the original message and encrypt each chunk separately with the authenticated cipher. An example of a scheme like that can be found in the DARE protocol used by the MinIO project, which you can read more about here: `https://bit.ly/crypto-dare` (it also includes a reference implementation in Go).

Ultimately, the choice of what mode of operation to use depends on your application, how the data is stored and/or transmitted, and whether you are hashing the data separately. If we were to make a very high-level recommendation, we would recommend the following:

- CBC should be your default mode of operation.
- GCM can be used when you're going to store the ciphertext in certain places, or transmit it through channels, where others could potentially alter your encrypted data.

Initialization vector

The last thing you need to know about AES is that in most modes of operation (including CBC and GCM), it requires an **initialization vector (IV)**.

An IV is a random sequence of bytes that should be regenerated every time you're encrypting a file. As a rule, you should **never reuse an IV**.

The size of the IV is fixed and independent of the size of the key, and it is as follows:

- 16 bytes for AES-CBC
- 12 bytes for AES-GCM

The IV does not need to be kept secret, and it's common to store the IV, in plaintext form, alongside the encrypted data (ciphertext), such as at the beginning of the encrypted stream.

Using AES with Node.js

The good news for us is that Node.js includes built-in support for AES in the `crypto` module, including hardware acceleration where available. The two main methods are `createCipheriv(algorithm, key, iv)`, for creating a cipher (for encrypting data), and `createDecipheriv(algorithm, key, iv)`, for creating a decipher (for decrypting data).

Both methods accept an algorithm as the first argument, which includes the key size and the mode of operation. Considering 128- or 256-bit keys, and CBC or GCM as the mode of operation, you have four options to choose from for the `algorithm` parameter: `aes-128-cbc`, `aes-256-cbc`, `aes-128-gcm`, or `aes-256-gcm`.

You can also see the full list of supported ciphers in your system by using `crypto.getCiphers()`, which may contain over a hundred different options (depending on the version of Node.js and the OpenSSL library linked to it), including legacy ones.

Example – AES-256-CBC

Let's look at an example of using **AES-CBC** with a 256-bit key to encrypt and then decrypt a message using Node.js:

4.1: Encryption and decryption with AES-256-CBC (aes-256-cbc.js)

```
const crypto = require('crypto')
const randomBytes = require('util')
    .promisify(crypto.randomBytes)
```

```
async function encrypt(key, plaintext) {
    const iv = await randomBytes(16)
    const cipher = crypto.createCipheriv('aes-256-cbc', key, iv)
    const encrypted = Buffer.concat([
        cipher.update(plaintext, 'utf8'),
        cipher.final()
    ])
    return Buffer.concat([iv, encrypted])
}

function decrypt(key, message) {
    const iv = message.slice(0, 16)
    const ciphertext = message.slice(16)
    const decipher = crypto.createDecipheriv('aes-256-cbc',
        key, iv)
    const decrypted = Buffer.concat([
        decipher.update(ciphertext, 'utf8'),
        decipher.final()
    ])

    return decrypted.toString('utf8')
}
```

We start the code by importing the `crypto` module. Just like we did in the previous chapters, we are using `util.promisify` to "modernize" some older methods, such as `crypto.randomBytes`, so that they return a `Promise` (which can be used in an async function with the `await` keyword).

In the preceding code, we have defined two functions:

- As its name suggests, `encrypt` is used to encrypt a plaintext message (a string) with a given 256-bit symmetric key (in a `Buffer` object), returning the ciphertext.

  The method begins by generating an IV as a random 16-byte sequence. Then, it creates a cipher (the object that will encrypt our data) with `createCipheriv`, using the key that was passed and the random IV.

Next, the code uses `cipher.update` to encrypt the message, and then signals that no more data is coming with `cipher.final` (you could invoke `cipher.update` to pass chunks of data as many times as you need, until you invoke `cipher.final`).

At the end of the function, we return the result, which is the concatenation of two buffers: the IV and the ciphertext. It's common practice to store the IV before the ciphertext.

- Conversely, the `decrypt` method performs the opposite operation, decrypting a ciphertext (in a `Buffer` object) with a given 256-bit symmetric key (again, as a `Buffer` argument), and returns the plaintext message as a string.

  Because we are storing the IV at the beginning of the encrypted message, the first thing we need to do is `slice` the `message` argument into two parts. The first 16 bytes are the IV, while the rest is the actual ciphertext.

  Next, we create a decipher with `createDecipheriv`, passing the key and the IV that was extracted from the beginning of the message. We then use the `decipher` object, just like we did with the cipher object in the previous method, invoking `decipher.update` with the ciphertext to decrypt and use `decipher.final` when we're done.

  Because the message that was encrypted at the beginning (with the `encrypt` function) was a string, the `decrypt` function returns the result as a string too, in its original UTF-8 representation.

Let's look at how we can use these functions. In this example, we are generating a new, random 256-bit key every time using the `crypto.randomBytes` method, which we encountered in *Chapter 2, Dealing with Binary and Random Data*. At the end of this chapter, we'll learn how to derive a key from a passphrase as well:

4.2: Example of using the AES-256-CBC functions

```
;(async () => {
    const plaintext = 'Hello world!'


    const key = await randomBytes(32)
    console.log('Key:', key.toString('base64'))


    const encrypted = await encrypt(key, plaintext)
    console.log('Encrypted message:', encrypted.
        toString('base64'))
```

```
      const decrypted = decrypt(key, encrypted)
      console.log('Decrypted message:', decrypted)
})()
```

In this case, we are wrapping our code in an async **Immediately-Invoked Function Expression (IIFE)** with `;(async () => { ... })()` so that we can use the `await` keyword.

After defining the plaintext we want to encrypt (in this simple example, the `Hello world!` string), we generate a random key of 32 bytes (256 bits).

Next, we encrypt the message and then decrypt it again to verify that the output matches the input.

In the console, you should see a result similar to this (but one that changes every time):

```
Key:
eydo/M0UBy62ipiqGn4bhUQsiA4HWJ0mVtdi4W72urQ=
Encrypted message: xwS/cTRCPgVoTeARmmbajlkUm4P2TC8mY9devEt+Kcw=
Decrypted message:
Hello world!
```

Example – AES-256-GCM

With Node.js, the code for encrypting and decrypting data with **AES-GCM** is similar to the one we saw moments ago for AES-CBC, but it has one important difference.

As we mentioned previously, AES-GCM is an authenticated cipher, which means that in addition to the ciphertext, it also returns an authentication tag that must be stored alongside the encrypted message and must be provided to the decipher. The decipher will need this tag to verify that the data that was decrypted is valid and was not tampered with.

Let's look at how the encrypt and decrypt functions we saw in the AES-256-CBC example need to be modified for AES-256-GCM, with the changes in bold:

4.3: Encryption and decryption with AES-256-GCM (aes-256-gcm.js)

```
const crypto = require('crypto')
const randomBytes = require('util')
    .promisify(crypto.randomBytes)
```

```
async function encrypt(key, plaintext) {
    const iv = await randomBytes(12)
    const cipher = crypto.createCipheriv('aes-256-gcm', key, iv)
    const encrypted = Buffer.concat([
        cipher.update(plaintext, 'utf8'),
        cipher.final()
    ])
    const tag = cipher.getAuthTag()
    return Buffer.concat([iv, tag, encrypted])
}

function decrypt(key, message) {
    const iv = message.slice(0, 12)
    const tag = message.slice(12, 28)
    const ciphertext = message.slice(28)
    const decipher = crypto.createDecipheriv('aes-256-gcm',
        key, iv)
    decipher.setAuthTag(tag)
    const decrypted = Buffer.concat([
        decipher.update(ciphertext, 'utf8'),
        decipher.final()
    ])
    return decrypted.toString('utf8')
}
```

The main differences from the previous example are as follows:

1. The IV for AES in GCM mode is 12 bytes long (rather than 16 in CBC mode).

2. The name of the cipher for the `crypto.createCipheriv` and `crypto.createDecipheriv` methods is `'aes-256-gcm'`.

3. After invoking `cipher.final` in the `encrypt` method, the `cipher` object contains the 16-byte authentication tag, which can be retrieved with `cipher.getAuthTag()`. We are storing this value in the resulting message, after the IV but before the ciphertext.

4.   Because we're storing the authentication tag at the beginning of the message, the `decipher` function needs to slice the encrypted message buffer into three parts: 12 bytes for the IV, 16 bytes for the authentication tag, with the rest being the ciphertext. After creating the `decipher` object, before we start passing the ciphertext to it, we need to invoke `decipher.setAuthTag` with the authentication tag.

You can invoke these functions using the very same code as in example *4.2*, which was for AES-CBC. This time, you'll see that your encrypted message is a little bit longer due to the presence of the authentication tag.

The main difference is that if you tried modifying the message encrypted with AES-CBC, the `decrypt` function would still succeed, but your output would look different from the input. However, with AES-GCM, you'd get a runtime exception, notifying you that the authentication tag does not match.

Using streams

Just like we saw with hashing in *Chapter 3*, *File and Password Hashing with Node.js*, the functions we have defined so far require loading the entire message in memory (in a string or `Buffer` object), so they're not suitable for encrypting large files.

Luckily, the `Cipher` and `Decipher` objects, which are returned by `crypto.createCipheriv` and `crypto.createDecipheriv`, respectively, can also be used with streams. This is particularly useful when you're trying to encrypt or decrypt large files (or messages of unknown length) because data will only be loaded in memory a chunk at a time.

When working with streams, using streaming ciphers such as AES with the GCM mode of operation is normally better. If you don't need authenticated encryption, the **CTR** (counter mode) is another streaming cipher that can be used as an option (*note that this is not one of the two modes we encountered, and recommended, earlier*).

The challenge with using authenticated ciphers and streams is that the authentication tag is generated by the cipher object once the entire file has been encrypted, yet it's needed by the decipher object before decryption can begin. This means that we won't be able to store the authentication tag at the beginning of the file, as we did previously (and like we're still doing for the IV) because we will have already flushed the data to the output stream. Instead, we need to keep the authentication tag separate from the file, such as in a database.

Let's look at an example of encrypting a file from disk, called `photo.jpg`, and writing the encrypted file in `photo.jpg.enc`, using AES-GCM. It then decrypts the file into `photo.jpg.orig` and uses the authentication tag to validate that the encrypted file was not tampered with. We'll start with the `encrypt` function:

4.4: Encrypting and decrypting a stream using AES-256-GCM (aes-stream.js)

```
const crypto = require('crypto')
const randomBytes = require('util')
    .promisify(crypto.randomBytes)


async function encrypt(key, source, destination) {
    const iv = await randomBytes(12)
    return new Promise((resolve, reject) => {
        const cipher = crypto.createCipheriv('aes-256-gcm',
            key, iv)
        cipher.on('end', () => {
            const tag = cipher.getAuthTag()
            resolve(tag)
        })
        cipher.on('error', (err) => {
            reject(err)
        })
        destination.write(iv)
        source.pipe(cipher).pipe(destination)
    })
}
```

Just like in the previous chapter's example, code that uses streams is a bit more convoluted, so let's go through this step by step:

1. The function accepts three parameters: `key` is the 256-bit symmetric key (as a `Buffer`) object, just like in the previous examples; `source` and `destination` are a readable stream to the input and a writable stream to the output, respectively.

2. We are wrapping the function's main code in a `Promise` object's callback so that we can use `encrypt` as an `async` function (and `await` on its result). This is similar to what we did in *Chapter 3, File and Password Hashing with Node.js*, when hashing a stream.

3. Inside the promise's callback, we create the `cipher` object, just like we did in the previous examples.

4. We attach a callback to when the cipher stream ends (`cipher.on('end',` `() => { … })`). Inside that, we retrieve the authentication tag and then we resolve the promise with the tag as a value. As you'll see in the following invocation example, this allows you to do `const tag = await encrypt(key,` `source, destination)` and have the tag returned at the end of the processing.

5. We also attach a callback to reject the promise when there's an error in the streams: `cipher.on('error', (err) => { reject(err) })`. This makes our `encrypt` function throw an exception in case of an error.

6. Because we want the output to contain our IV (which we generated at the start of the function) at the beginning, we write that to the destination stream before anything else with `destination.write(iv)`.

7. Lastly, we read and process the data from the `source` stream, piping it into the `cipher` object first (which acts as a transform stream that encrypts the data) and then piping that into the `destination` stream so that it can be written to the destination (for example, a file).

Similarly, we can define a `decrypt` function that, still working with streams, does the inverse operation:

4.5: (Continued) Encrypting and decrypting a stream using AES-256-GCM (aes-stream.js)

```
async function decrypt(key, tag, source, destination) {
    const iv = await new Promise((resolve) => {
        const cb = () => {
            const iv = source.read(12)
            source.off('readable', cb)
            return resolve(iv)
        }
        source.on('readable', cb)
    })
    if (!iv) {
        throw Error('iv is null')
    }

    return new Promise((resolve, reject) => {
```

```
        const decipher = crypto.createDecipheriv('aes-256-gcm',
            key, iv)
        decipher.setAuthTag(tag)
        decipher.on('end', () => {
            resolve()
        })
        decipher.on('error', (err) => {
            reject(err)
        })
        source.pipe(decipher).pipe(destination)
    })
}
```

The decrypt function accepts four arguments: the key (the same 256-bit symmetric key that was used to encrypt the file), the authentication tag (as returned by the encrypt function), the source stream that reads the ciphertext (which begins with the IV), and the destination stream where the plaintext is written to.

Admittedly, this looks even scarier, but we can analyze it by splitting it into two parts:

- The first half of the decrypt function's goal is to extract the IV from the stream. Remember that our encrypt function puts the IV at the beginning of the stream, so the first Promise object we create and await on is meant to read the first 12 bytes of the stream (and no more than 12 bytes) and get the IV.

  At a high level, the promise's callback works by attaching a handler that is invoked when the source stream has data available to read. That handler reads 12 bytes exactly (and nothing more, to not consume the ciphertext in the stream), which is then used to resolve the promise. The handler detaches itself from the stream once the IV has been read.

- The second half of the function should look similar to what we did with the encrypt function moments ago. The differences are that we are creating a Decipher object with createDecipheriv (rather than a Cipher) and passing the authentication tag to it before we begin piping the data to be decrypted. Once the stream ends (and all the data has been fully decrypted), the Promise is resolved with no value; in case of error, it's rejected instead.

To invoke these two functions, we can use the following code:

4.6: Invoking the functions that use streams to encrypt and decrypt data with AES

```
const fs = require('fs')
;(async function() {
    const key = await randomBytes(32)
    console.log('Key:', key.toString('base64'))
    const testFile = 'photo.jpg'
    let tag
    {
        const inFile = fs.createReadStream(testFile)
        const outFile = fs.createWriteStream(testFile + '.enc')
        tag = await encrypt(key, inFile, outFile)
        console.log('File was encrypted; authentication tag:',
            tag.toString('base64'))
    }
    {
        const inFile = fs.createReadStream(testFile + '.enc')
        const outFile = fs.createWriteStream(testFile +
            '.orig')
        await decrypt(key, tag, inFile, outFile)
        console.log('File was decrypted successfully')
    }
})()
```

In this example, we are encrypting the photo.jpg file using a randomly generated key every time. Let's take a look:

1. First, we encrypt the file. We create a readable stream to photo.jpg (inFile) and a writable stream to photo.jpg.enc (outFile, where we want the ciphertext to be written to). Then, we invoke the encrypt function asynchronously by passing the key, the input stream, and the output stream. The result of the function is the authentication tag (a Buffer object) that we display on the terminal. In a real application, you'd want to store the tag somewhere alongside your encrypted file, for example: in a database, in an index file, in a separate metadata file, or other places.

2. In the next step, we reverse the operation and decrypt the photo back into a file called photo.jpg.orig. This time, the readable stream, inFile, is reading photo.jpg.enc (the ciphertext), while the writable stream, outFile, points to our target file: photo.jpg.orig. Then, we invoke the decrypt function asynchronously, passing the key (the same as we did previously), the authentication tag returned by encrypt, and the input and output streams.

After running the preceding code, you'll see that you have two more files in your folder alongside photo.jpg: photo.jpg.enc and photo.jpg.orig. The photo.jpg.enc file is encrypted, so it will look like a blob of random data; however, if everything went well, photo.jpg.orig should look the same as the original file.

To check that the files are identical, you can hash them, as we saw in *Chapter 3, File and Password Hashing with Node.js*:

```
photo.jpg f14fe4c5fc04089cba31559e9ed88cf268fb61f43a15e9b3bb94
ff63ac57b5b2
```

```
photo.jpg.orig f14fe4c5fc04089cba31559e9ed88cf268fb61f43a15e9b3
bb94ff63ac57b5b2
```

The actual checksums will be different for your files, but the important part is that they match! This means that the file was encrypted and then decrypted successfully, and the preceding code is correct.

As we mentioned earlier, Node.js offers built-in support for many more symmetric ciphers besides AES. Many of them are legacy ones and are only offered for compatibility reasons, but others can be valid alternatives, depending on your scenario. In the next section, we'll look at one of those.

Symmetric encryption with ChaCha20-Poly1305

ChaCha20 is a more recent symmetric cipher designed by Daniel J. Bernstein in the mid-'00s. It's often used together with the Poly1305 hashing function (in this case, it's also called "message authentication code"), which was designed by the same cryptographer. The result of the combination of the two is the **ChaCha20-Poly1305** authenticated stream cipher.

We talked about authenticated stream ciphers in the previous section when referring to AES-GCM: functionally, ChaCha20-Poly1305 serves the same purpose. Even in practice, they are used very similarly, as you'll see in the samples in this section.

ChaCha20-Poly1305 has been seeing an increase in interest and popularity in recent years since it's now implemented by a variety of applications and, more frequently, as a cipher for the TLS protocol (used by HTTPS). For example, Google offers support for it in all of its online services and in the Android operating system. Cloudflare, whose CDN protects a large number of websites, has enabled it for all of their customers too.

Let's be clear on one thing: the reasons behind the interest in ChaCha20-Poly1305 have nothing to do with security. At the time of writing, both ChaCha20-Poly1305 and AES-GCM offer the same level of security, given keys of the same size, with neither of the two having any publicly-known security vulnerability.

However, on devices where hardware-based AES acceleration is not available, ChaCha20-Poly1305 is known to be significantly faster. While most, if not all, modern PCs and laptops have CPUs with hardware acceleration, the same isn't always true for mobile and embedded devices, so offering those clients the choice of a faster software-based cipher can make a difference.

Example usage with Node.js

With Node.js, support for ChaCha20-Poly1305 is available in the `crypto` module starting with version 11.2, when compiled against a recent-enough version of OpenSSL. Technically speaking, the version of ChaCha20-Poly1305 that's implemented in Node.js is the one compatible with RFC 7539 (also called the IETF variant). To use it, we can implement our usual `encrypt` and `decrypt` functions, which look very similar to the ones we wrote for AES-GCM:

4.7: Encryption and decryption with ChaCha20-Poly1305 (chacha20-po-ly1305.js)

```
const crypto = require('crypto')
const randomBytes = require('util')
    .promisify(crypto.randomBytes)


async function encrypt(key, plaintext) {
    const nonce = await randomBytes(12)
    const cipher = crypto.createCipheriv('chacha20-poly1305',
        key, nonce, {
        authTagLength: 16
    })
    const encrypted = Buffer.concat([
        cipher.update(plaintext, 'utf8'),
```

```
        cipher.final()
    ])
    const tag = cipher.getAuthTag()
    return Buffer.concat([nonce, tag, encrypted])
}


function decrypt(key, message) {
    const nonce = message.slice(0, 12)
    const tag = message.slice(12, 28)
    const ciphertext = message.slice(28)
    const decipher = crypto.createDecipheriv('chacha20-
        poly1305', key, nonce, {
        authTagLength: 16
    })
    decipher.setAuthTag(tag)
    const decrypted = Buffer.concat([
        decipher.update(ciphertext, 'utf8'),
        decipher.final()
    ])
    return decrypted.toString('utf8')
}
```

The differences between the functions that we used for AES-GCM are highlighted in the preceding code:

1. The identifier for the algorithm in the `crypto.createCipheriv` and `crypto.createDecipheriv` methods is `'chacha20-poly1305'`.

2. While AES-GCM requires a 96-bit (12 bytes) IV, ChaCha20-Poly1305 requires a **nonce** of the same length. While conceptually different, nonces are 12 random bytes that are generated and used the same way as IVs are in our code.

3. Lastly, the `crypto.createCipheriv` and `crypto.createDecipheriv` methods require a fourth argument, which is a JavaScript object containing `{authTagLength: 16}` to indicate that we want a 128-bit (16 bytes) authentication tag.

The rest of the code and the way it's invoked remains unchanged from the preceding examples for AES-GCM.

When to use ChaCha20-Poly1305 or AES-GCM

As we mentioned previously, AES-GCM and ChaCha20-Poly1305 offer the same security, but the latter is **faster when hardware acceleration is not available**.

This makes the ChaCha20-Poly1305 cipher very interesting to implement on HTTPS web servers when you want to support mobile clients, especially lower-end ones that may have CPUs without AES acceleration or embedded systems such as **Internet of Things (IoT)** devices.

However, these situations are generally in the infrastructure realm and not something that is of relevance to your application code. That is, to enable ChaCha20-Poly1305 as a cipher for TLS, you generally need to tweak your web server or proxy configuration (such as Nginx) rather than make a code change in your app. With Node.js, when your application is directly exposed to the Internet (without using reverse proxies, CDNs, and so on), ChaCha20-Poly1305 is already enabled by default by the built-in HTTPS server, so there's nothing you need to do there.

As a developer building an app that runs on top of Node.js, then, there are only a few situations when choosing ChaCha20-Poly1305 over AES may make sense:

- When you're adding encryption to a CLI app written in Node.js that may be run on a variety of clients, including those without hardware-accelerated AES.

- When you're building a server-side app that will run on a system without hardware acceleration for AES. While this is exceedingly rare with "regular" servers or cloud infrastructure, a notable exception is when you are running your app on a Raspberry Pi (at the time of writing, the latest model is *4 Model B*, which does not support hardware-accelerated AES).

- When you need compatibility with applications that are running on systems that don't have hardware AES acceleration. For example, if your server-side Node.js app receives encrypted data from low-powered IoT devices, then encrypting that with ChaCha20-Poly1305 may give you better performance overall than using AES-GCM.

With this, we have learned about all the most important symmetric ciphers. Now, it's time to look into the other core part of symmetric cryptography: keys.

Key derivation

In all our examples so far, we've generated a new key every time by grabbing a random sequence of bytes from `crypto.randomBytes`. While a random key always gives the best security, in many situations we need to be able to have a memorable (or at least, human-readable) **passphrase to derive the symmetric keys from**.

As we mentioned previously, AES requires a 128-, 192-, or 256-bit key, which means 16, 24, or 32 bytes. You might be tempted to grab a string of 16 characters and call it a 128-bit key, such as `thisismykey12345`... however, that would be a **really bad** idea. Despite being 128 bits in length, it is only made up of lowercase letters and numbers, so its entropy is significantly lower than 128 bits: in fact, this has only about 60 bits of entropy, which means that it can be cracked relatively quickly with a brute-force attack (see *Chapter 3, File and Password Hashing with Node.js,* for an explanation on entropy).

However, all is not lost, and we can stretch passphrases into safe keys by using a **Key Derivation Function** (**KDF**), as we saw in *Chapter 3, File and Password Hashing with Node.js* (*as I warned you, hashes are omnipresent!*).

In particular, in that chapter, we mentioned that two hashing functions were well-suited to be used for key derivation: **Argon2**, or if that's not available, **scrypt**. As we explained there, KDFs are deliberately slow to compute, so they are able to significantly increase the cost (time and/or resources) for an attacker trying to perform a brute-force attack on a low-entropy input such as a passphrase.

Because we discussed hashing functions at length in the previous chapter, we will not cover them again here; instead, we'll just look at an example of using Argon2 (in the Argon2id variant) to derive a key from a passphrase.

This will be very similar to the code in the previous chapter, but this time, we're requesting the raw bytes returned by Argon2, rather than a base64-encoded hash that contains the parameters too. To ensure consistency and repeatability, we are also explicitly passing some salt and all the parameters for Argon2:

4.8: Deriving keys using Argon2 (argon2-kdf.js)

```
// From NPM: https://www.npmjs.com/package/argon2
const argon2 = require('argon2')


function deriveKey(passphrase, salt, length) {
    try {
        const params = {
            raw: true,
            hashLength: length,
            salt: salt,
            type: argon2.argon2id,
            timeCost: 3,
            memoryCost: 4096,
            parallelism: 1,
```

```
            version: 0x13,
        }

        const result = await argon2.hash(passphrase, params)
        return result
    }
    catch (err) {
        console.error('An internal error occurred: ', err)
    }
}
```

The deriveKey function returns a Promise that resolves with a Buffer with a symmetric key, and it accepts three arguments:

- passphrase is a string with the passphrase to derive the key from.

- salt is a Buffer object that's used as salt and should be 16 bytes in length. The salt (which is not a secret) should be stored somewhere such as in a database and optimally it should be unique for each passphrase.

- length is the length of the key to return, in bytes. It should be 16 for a 128-bit key or 32 for a 256-bit key.

Note that in the parameters for the hash, we are specifying raw: true, which makes argon2.hash return just the hash as a Buffer object, without encoding it as base64 and without prepending the parameters. We need just the hash here!

Additionally, as you can see here, and unlike in the example shown in *Chapter 3, File and Password Hashing with Node.js*, this time we are being explicit about the parameters that are used in the argon2.hash invocation rather than accepting all the defaults. This is necessary because we want to make sure that for each invocation, with the same pair of inputs for passphrase and salt, the result is the same. We can't rely on the defaults that are baked into the library in case they change in the future (which is not a problem when we ask argon2.hash to return a string, because it stores the parameters it used at the beginning of the hash).

Tuning the Argon2 Parameters

The parameters we used here for timeCost, memoryCost, and parallelism control the "cost" of running the Argon2 KDF. The costlier each invocation of Argon2 is, the higher the effort (time and/or energy) is for an attacker to break your symmetric key, so the stronger the protection is against brute-force attacks. In your application, you may want to tune those parameters so that the function takes as much time as you're willing to tolerate for your solution.

You can run the preceding function asynchronously with the `await` keyword. For example, to generate a 256-bit key, you can use the following code:

```
const key = await deriveKey(passphrase, salt, 32)
```

The function is deterministic, so given the same passphrase, salt, and length, you should always get the same result. For example, let's say you have these inputs (and the parameters unchanged from code sample 4.8):

```
;(async function() {
    const passphrase = 'correct horse battery staple'
    const salt = Buffer.from('WiHmGLjgzYESy3eAW45W0Q==',
        'base64')
    const key128 = await deriveKey(passphrase, salt, 16)
    console.log('128-bit key:', key128.toString('base64'))
    const key256 = await deriveKey(passphrase, salt, 32)
    console.log('256-bit key:', key256.toString('base64'))
})()
```

The result is always (and on every machine) as follows:

```
128-bit key: McvSLprU4zfh1kcVOeR40g==
256-bit key: oQumof86t+UlE6yBPCbbl06IcPmrL8qHj/jucYIxJFw=
```

> **Using scrypt as a KDF**
>
> In *Chapter 3, File and Password Hashing with Node.js*, we mentioned that scrypt is another valid KDF and that it can be used when Argon2 is not available. The `crypto.scrypt` function, which is available in Node.js already, returns a raw `Buffer` object that can be used as a symmetric key and has an optional parameter that can be used to tune its cost. You can read more about this in the Node.js documentation: `https://bit.ly/crypto-scrypt`

Reusing keys

So long as the IV is random and unique for each invocation, it's ok to reuse the same key more than once.

However, especially with AES in GCM and CTR modes, you should **never use the same IV twice with the same key**. Doing that may **expose your encryption key** to an attacker.

With GCM mode, the IV is relatively small at only 12 bytes, so the chances of a collision occurring are relatively high when the same key is reused many times. Because of that, if you're able to generate a new key every time, such as for every new file, it would be a good idea to do so.

When you use a KDF to derive a key, you can, for example, use a different random salt for each file, and then store that salt alongside your file (as we mentioned previously, it's ok for the salt to be public). Using a different salt allows you to get a different key every time, eliminating the risk of reusing an IV.

Deriving keys from passphrases is an incredibly common operation for applications that leverage cryptography. However, when encrypting data with keys derived from user-supplied passphrases, there's one more thing we need to consider, as we'll see in the next section.

Wrapping keys and best practices for encrypting large documents

In the previous section, we learned how symmetric keys are often derived from passphrases. Encrypting data with a passphrase or passcode that the user memorizes (or stores in a password wallet) is at the core of many, many solutions that leverage cryptography, such as to encrypt documents or files. The next time you unlock your laptop with a passphrase or your phone with a PIN, think about the key derivation functions and ciphers that are being executed!

By reading this chapter up to this point, you should already be able to build an application like the one we just described with Node.js. For example, you could use Argon2 to derive a key from a passphrase submitted by the user, and then use AES-GCM to encrypt and decrypt files.

However, passphrases are not static. That is to say that users do change their passphrases, sometimes because they want to rotate them, or sometimes because their previous one was compromised (a surprisingly frequent occurrence nowadays!).

Sadly, when a passphrase changes, the encryption key that's derived from it changes too, which means you'll need to re-encrypt every single document that used that key. If there are lots of those documents and/or they are large, that can take a lot of time!

To avoid having to re-encrypt everything when a user changes their passphrase, the usual scheme involves encrypting each file with a separate, random key, which is in turn encrypted with the key derived from the user's passphrase.

> **Terminology**
>
> In this section, you'll frequently read the expressions **key wrapping** and **key unwrapping**. These are just two fancier names that refer to the operations of encrypting and decrypting keys, respectively. When you encrypt another key, you are wrapping it; you can then unwrap it to get the original key.
>
> As for the keys, there's no strict naming convention about what the one that's used to encrypt data is called, but in this section, will refer to it as a **user key** (**UK**). Instead, the key that's used to wrap the other user key is usually called a **key encryption key** (**KEK**) or a **wrapping key** (**WK**).

AES Key Wrap

When you're choosing what algorithm to use to wrap keys, any symmetric (or even asymmetric) cipher would work (ideally you'd want to use an authenticated cipher). In fact, at the byte level, keys are not unlike any other message your applications will encrypt!

Nevertheless, cryptographers have created a class of algorithms that are specifically optimized for wrapping and unwrapping other keys. Unlike the ciphers that we've seen earlier in this chapter, such as AES-GCM or ChaCha20-Poly1305, they aim to be able to offer integrity without the use of any nonce or random IV.

AES Key Wrap, also called **AES-KW**, is a mode of operation of the AES cipher that is optimized for wrapping symmetric keys. It's defined in RFC 3394 and it's widely available, including in the Node.js `crypto` module.

In the following code samples, we'll be using AES-KW for wrapping and unwrapping keys. You'll see that its use is almost identical to how we implemented solutions based on AES-CBC, with just two differences. First, the name of the cipher (for `createCipheriv` and `createDecipheriv`) is the odd-looking `'id-aes256-wrap'`. Second, the IV that's used is defined by the RFC and it's a fixed value; that is, `0xA6A6A6A6A6A6A6A6` (hex-encoded).

Wrapping user keys

Let's start by looking at the high-level description of the algorithm.

When your application is started for the first time – or, in a multi-user system, when a new user account is created – you must do the following:

1. Prompt the user for a passphrase, then derive a symmetric key from that using the KDF of your choice, such as Argon2id – this is the **wrapping key** (**WK**).

2. Calculate the hash of the passphrase, which we'll use to verify that the user entered the correct passphrase when they try to encrypt or decrypt data.

If you're using a KDF such as Argon2id, a safe and convenient option is to ask the function to generate 32 more bytes of data, for a total of 64 bytes: the first 32 bytes are the WK, while the rest is used as a hash to verify the passphrase. This is done by setting `hashLength: 64` in the parameters for the Argon2 function's invocation, as we saw previously.

3. Generate a random key, such as a random 32-byte sequence, which will be used as the **user key (UK)**.

4. Using the WK, wrap the UK by encrypting it with the symmetric key encryption algorithm.

5. Store the wrapped key and the password hash with the user's profile in your application.

Once you have generated the UK, then wrapped and stored it with the user's profile, you can use that to encrypt and decrypt data as needed:

1. Prompt the user for the passphrase again.

2. Rerun the KDF to obtain the WK and calculate the hash of the passphrase – as we saw previously, this can be done in the same step.

3. Compare the passphrase hashes to ensure they match: the one you just generated and the one stored in the user's profile. If they don't match, stop here and return an error.

4. Using the WK derived from the passphrase, unwrap the key that is stored in the user's profile. That key (which should only be kept in memory for the time it's needed) is the UK and can be used to encrypt and decrypt data.

You can find an example of implementing this in the `key-wrap.js` file in this book's GitHub repository, in the `ch4-symmetric-encryption` folder. While we won't be able to analyze it in detail here, the code is fully commented on and shows an implementation for all the steps described here.

With a solution like this, if the user decides to change their passphrase, then you need to repeat the steps you performed when creating a new user account but reusing the existing user key (UK) instead of generating a new (random) one. This means creating a new salt, deriving a new wrapping key (WK) and passphrase hash, and re-encrypting the original user key (UK). You will get a new wrapped key, but because the UK hasn't changed, you won't need to re-encrypt every single file that the user stored.

> **Using a Different Key for Each File**
>
> In the examples in this section, we've assumed that each user has one and only one UK, which is used to encrypt and decrypt every file the user owns. While this approach is perfectly fine for encrypting data that only one user can see, it makes it challenging to share files with others.
>
> One common solution to this problem (whose implementation we're leaving as an exercise for you) is to encrypt each file with a third key, which we can call the **file key (FK)**. Each file you encrypt uses a different, random FK. Let's assume that two users want to have access to that file, each one having their own UK: we'll call those UK_1 and UK_2 (and both those UKs are stored in a database wrapped with the respective user's wrapping key). You will then wrap the FK twice, with UK_1 and UK_2. This gives both users access to that shared file and that only, without having to know the other person's UK.

Summary

In this chapter, we learned about encrypting data with a symmetric cipher, starting with AES. After learning about how to use AES, including how to choose the size of the key, how to select a mode of operation (especially CBC and GCM), and how to generate an IV, we saw code samples for encrypting and decrypting data and streams with AES using Node.js. We then learned about ChaCha20-Poly1305, another symmetric stream cipher that's similar to AES-GCM.

Next, we explained how to derive encryption keys from a passphrase, stretching lower-entropy strings into safer keys for usage with symmetric ciphers. We saw examples of doing that with Argon2.

Finally, we learned how keys can be wrapped (encrypted), and why doing so can help solve real-world problems when applications use keys derived from passphrases to encrypt and decrypt users' data.

The next chapter will be the first one that covers the other kind of ciphers – asymmetric ones. We'll learn how to use public-key cryptography with algorithms such as RSA to encrypt and decrypt data.

5
Using Asymmetric and Hybrid Encryption in Node.js

In the previous chapter, *Chapter 4, Symmetric Encryption in Node.js*, we looked at how to protect the confidentiality of data by encrypting it using symmetric ciphers. Algorithms like the ones we used (AES and ChaCha20-Poly1305) are highly secure and fast, but they use a single key (in this case, a **shared key**) for both encryption and decryption. Consequently, to send an encrypted message to another person, both parties need to know the shared key too: safely transmitting that over an insecure channel (such as the internet) can become a problem.

As we briefly mentioned in the previous chapter, for these situations, it's often convenient to leverage a different class of cryptographic operations: **asymmetric cryptography**, also called **public-key cryptography**, since it uses two kinds of keys – a public key and a private key. RSA is one of the most popular and widely adopted algorithms for public-key encryption and is the first one we'll look at in this chapter.

Because public-key cryptography is very slow and can only encrypt small amounts of data, in practice, most implementations rely on **hybrid cryptosystems**, in which the data is encrypted using a symmetric cipher (for example, AES). Then, public-key cryptography is used to securely exchange the shared key. In this chapter, we'll look at how to implement a hybrid scheme with RSA, and then we'll learn how to use Elliptic-Curve Cryptography (ECC) to perform a key agreement (using the **Elliptic-curve Diffie-Hellman** protocol, or **ECDH**).

In this chapter, we're going to cover the following main topics:

- An overview of public-key and hybrid cryptosystems
- Loading and exporting private and public keys with Node.js, and the PEM format
- Using RSA with Node.js, also to perform hybrid encryption
- Using ECDH for key agreement and the ECIES hybrid scheme with Node.js

Technical requirements

You can find the code files for this chapter on GitHub at `https://bit.ly/crypto-ch5`.

Understanding public-key and hybrid cryptosystems

Before we dive into the code and learn about using asymmetric and hybrid encryption schemes with Node.js, it's worth spending a few moments understanding why we need these algorithms, what kinds of real-world problems we're trying to solve, and how they work, at least conceptually.

The need for public-key cryptography

We briefly mentioned this in the first section of *Chapter 4*, *Symmetric Encryption in Node.js*, when we explained the difference between symmetric and asymmetric ciphers, and how the latter helps solve the problem of transmitting keys to another party over an insecure channel.

For example, let's imagine that Alice needs to send Bob some confidential information via email (*cryptographers have a predilection for those two names when they want to describe a situation with two parties*); this is a very common problem in real life and is something you may have had to deal with yourself too on occasion!

Email is a notoriously insecure channel, given that messages are not encrypted: even though it's common to use **Transport Layer Security** (**TLS**) to protect the communication between email clients and servers, the actual messages are not end-to-end encrypted, and the server and any client can see them in full (recall the various layers of encryption we saw in *Chapter 1, Cryptography for Developers*).

Many people in Alice's situation would solve this problem by creating an encrypted ZIP file or using the built-in encryption features of Microsoft Office apps, PDF files, and so on. In all those cases, the solutions use symmetric ciphers with a key derived from a password. While doing this effectively protects the data that's sent over email, it leaves the problem of sharing the symmetric key (that is, the password) on the table. Because having both the encrypted file and the key is necessary *and* sufficient to decrypt the data, those two should not be sent together in the same email. Otherwise, an attacker who breaks into one of the two persons' inboxes would have a really easy time gaining full access to the confidential information.

A common workaround is to share the passphrase using another channel – for example, a phone call or an instant message; before the advent of public-key cryptography, people sometimes sent pre-shared passphrases via courier to others to exchange encrypted messages in the future. As a fun fact, the "red telephone" that was used during the Cold War for communication between Washington and Moscow used an encryption system in which the key was encoded on a tape that was delivered via embassies. While all these ideas could work, and they do offer protection against an attacker that is intercepting a single communication channel only, they're inefficient: they require the two parties to have multiple ways to communicate with each other, they introduce more complex processes, and they can be very slow – especially when paper or tapes are involved!

All told, although it may be ok for Alice to share the password of the encrypted ZIP with her friend Bob over the phone, this is not something that scales when the two parties don't know each other, or when the exchange needs to be fast and/or short-lived. Think, for example, of browsing the web using TLS, where a client and a server need to agree on an encryption key "instantaneously."

Public-key cryptography solves these problems (and more) by making it possible for Alice and Bob to each have a key pair consisting of a private and public key.

One of the most common algorithms that's used for asymmetric encryption is **RSA**, whose name is the acronym of the last names of those who invented it in 1977: Ron Rivest, Adi Shamir, and Leonard Adleman.

Using an algorithm like RSA, messages are *encrypted using the public key* and can be *decrypted only using the private one*. Going back to our example, using RSA, Bob would first share his public key with Alice, who would then use it to encrypt her message. Once the message has been encrypted, only Bob can decrypt it, using his private key.

As we mentioned in the previous chapter, asymmetric encryption is not widely understood by the general public, and yet virtually every person in the world uses it – even if unknowingly – daily. Protocols such as TLS (which underpins HTTPS, among others) are based on public-key cryptography, and so are encrypted messaging apps (such as Signal, Telegram, or WhatsApp) and email protocols (GPG, S/MIME), remote access protocols or VPNs (such as SSH, IPSec, and OpenVPN), and even cryptocurrencies.

Public-key cryptography has a few interesting properties:

- Each party has a pair of keys: a public and a private one. As we mentioned previously, one uses the public key to encrypt a message, while the private key is used to decrypt it.

- It's easy to compute the public key from the private one. However, it's mathematically impossible to go the other way around: given a public key, you cannot derive the private one.

- Given these two points, it's not only perfectly safe to share your public key, but it's necessary to allow others to encrypt messages before sending them to you. For example, solutions such as GPG (which allows you to send encrypted emails, among other things) maintain a publicly searchable database of everyone's public key around the world.

In addition to protecting confidentiality with data encryption, public-key cryptography has a few other applications too. The biggest one of those is computing **digital signatures**, which we'll learn about in *Chapter 6, Digital Signatures with Node.js and Trust*.

Hybrid cryptosystems

While public-key ciphers such as RSA can be used to encrypt data, they're generally very slow. Compared to symmetric ciphers, like those we saw in the previous chapter, asymmetric ones can be orders of magnitude slower as they are based on more computationally intensive algorithms.

In the case of RSA, then, there's an additional limitation in that the amount of data that can be encrypted is small: depending on the key size and how the algorithms are used, the longest message that can be encrypted might be 200 bytes or less.

In practice, then, most solutions that are designed to encrypt data leveraging public-key cryptography implement **hybrid cryptosystems**. The message is first encrypted with a symmetric cipher such as AES, using a randomly generated key, and then the symmetric key is wrapped (that is, encrypted) using an asymmetric algorithm such as RSA.

Hybrid approaches like these offer the best of both worlds, allowing arbitrary amounts of data to be encrypted quickly, while still leveraging public-key algorithms to allow two parties to safely exchange the symmetric key.

In this chapter, we'll look at two examples of building hybrid cryptosystems: by performing a key change with RSA and by using an ECDH key agreement (based on ECC).

Before we get into the details of using those algorithms, however, we need to understand how public and private keys can be generated, encoded, and exchanged or stored.

Loading, exporting, and encoding public and private keys

When you're working with asymmetric ciphers, one of the first problems you'll need to deal with is managing public and private keys, including loading and saving them to files or transmitting them to another person.

Both public and private keys contain long sequences of bytes. In the case of RSA, for example, private keys contain at least two main factors: a modulus and a secret exponent, each one long 2048, 3072, or 4096 bits (256, 384, or 512 bytes). Being binary data, they are not representable in a human-readable format, cannot be copied/pasted easily, and so on. To make handling keys more convenient, thus, we usually encode them.

Encoding keys as PEM

There are multiple formats for encoding private and public keys, but the de facto standard is DER-encoded ASN.1 stored in a PEM block, or simply "PEM format." Without getting into the details, which are not useful for our discussion, a PEM file contains two "comments" delimiting a block of base64-encoded data, which is the ASN.1 data structure encoded as DER. To oversimplify this, think of ASN.1 as an index of all the supported fields and their values, and then DER as a binary encoding format to represent those data structures. This very high-level explanation is provided just in case you stumbled upon those acronyms in the documentation for certain APIs.

A PEM file looks like this:

```
-----BEGIN FOO-----
(Block of base64-encoded data)
-----END FOO-----
```

Here, FOO indicates the type of data contained in the block; for example, PUBLIC KEY or PRIVATE KEY. Also, please note that the number of dashes before and after, which is always five.

For example, a PEM-encoded public RSA key looks like this (the middle of the key was truncated for brevity):

```
-----BEGIN PUBLIC KEY-----
MIICIjANBgkqhkiG9w0BAQEFAAOCAg8AMIICCgKCAgEAmrFHgesrpk/28b
[...]
JOFXV5F6Otx0rRZLHf6jEQECAwEAAQ==
-----END PUBLIC KEY-----
```

PEM format can be used to represent both public and private keys, of any algorithm, including RSA and elliptic curves.

There are three main standards you need to be aware of when working with PEM-encoded keys:

- PKCS#1 is the older standard and supports RSA keys only. PEM-encoded PKCS#1 files begin with BEGIN RSA PRIVATE KEY or BEGIN RSA PUBLIC KEY (note the "RSA" token) for private and public keys, respectively.

- PKCS#8 is used to encode **private** keys of any kind (including elliptic curves). PKCS#8 PEM blocks begin with BEGIN PRIVATE KEY (without the "RSA" token).

  Note that PKCS#8 private keys can optionally be encrypted too, by using a passphrase. In this case, the PEM blocks begin with BEGIN ENCRYPTED PRIVATE KEY. Encrypted keys are supported by Node.js too.

- For **public** keys of any kind, we can use the X.509 format (called SPKI in Node.js and PKIX in other places). Those PEM blocks start with BEGIN PUBLIC KEY.

Note that the PEM format is used to encode other kinds of information, including certificates, which we'll cover more in detail in *Chapter 6, Digital Signatures with Node.js and Trust*.

Reading and exporting keys

The crypto module in Node.js contains all the functions we need to load, manage, encode, and export public and private keys. Internally, keys – both public and private – are represented in crypto.KeyObject objects.

You can load a private key with the `crypto.createPrivateKey(key)` method. To load a plaintext PEM key, you can pass its content as a string (or `Buffer` object) directly as the `key` argument, like so:

```
const privateKeyObject = crypto.createPrivateKey(
    fs.readFileSync('private.pem')
)
```

If your PKCS#8 key is encrypted, you need to pass the key and the passphrase in an object as the `key` argument, like so:

```
const privateKeyObject = crypto.createPrivateKey({
    key: fs.readFileSync('private.pem'),
    passphrase: 'foo'
})
```

Similarly, to load a public key, you can use the `crypto.createPublicKey(key)` method. Because public keys cannot be encrypted, the only signature of this method that is of interest to us is the one where the `key` argument is a string or `Buffer` object containing our public key:

```
const publicKeyObject = crypto.createPublicKey(
    fs.readFileSync('public.pem')
)
```

Because, as you will recall, it's always possible to derive a public key from a private one (but not vice versa), you can also pass a private key file (that is, `private.pem` in our example) to `crypto.createPublicKey`, to load the public part of the key only.

Also, note that Node.js can automatically parse PEM-encoded keys, regardless of the standard that's used for encoding the key (such as PKCS#1, PKCS#8, or SPKI).

Lastly, objects of the `crypto.KeyObject` type – both those containing public and private keys – offer the `export(options)` method, which, as its name suggests, is used to export the key.

For **private** keys, the `options` argument is a dictionary with the following keys:

- `format`: While there are a couple of other options, we're always going to use `'pem'` here.

- `Type`: This can be `'pkcs8'` (recommended for most cases) or `'pkcs1'` (for RSA keys only).

- If you want to encrypt your private key, you can also set the `passphrase` and `cipher` options. The value of `cipher` must be a string with the name of a supported cipher, as we saw in *Chapter 4, Symmetric Encryption in Node.js*; for example, `'aes-256-cbc'`.

For **public** keys, the `options` dictionary can contain the following keys:

- `format`: Just like we did previously, we're always going to use `'pem'` as the format.
- `type`: This can be `'spki'` (recommended) or `'pkcs1'` (for RSA keys only).

PKCS#12 (PFX)

Another format you may need to be aware of is PKCS#12, also called PFX (from the name of the prior version of the standard). These files can encode both public and private keys, as well as certificates, in a format that is different from PEM. Of little relevance on *nix (Linux, macOS, and so on) systems and applications, PFX is notably the most widely used standard in Microsoft Windows for dealing with keys and certificates. These files usually have the `.p12` or `.pfx` extension.

Node.js does not support PKCS#12 natively, but you can find third-party packages on NPM to read or write those keys. Alternatively, they can be converted into PEM using tools such as OpenSSL.

Now that we've learned about keys, it's time to start using them to encrypt and decrypt data, starting with using RSA.

Using RSA with Node.js

We're finally ready to start writing some code to use public-key cryptography with Node.js!

In this section, we're going to learn how to generate RSA key pairs in Node.js and encrypt and decrypt messages with RSA. We'll then look at how to create a hybrid scheme based on RSA and a symmetric cipher such as AES to encrypt messages of any length.

Generating an RSA key pair

You can generate an RSA key pair with Node.js using the `crypto.generateKeyPair` function, as shown in this example:

5.1: Generate an RSA key pair (rsa-gen-keypair.js)

```
const crypto = require('crypto')
```

```
const fs = require('fs')
const util = require('util')
const generateKeyPair = util.promisify(crypto.generateKeyPair)
const writeFile = util.promisify(fs.writeFile)

;(async function() {
    const keyPair = await generateKeyPair('rsa', {
        modulusLength: 4096,
    })
    const privateKey = keyPair.privateKey.export({
        type: 'pkcs8',
        format: 'pem'
    })
    await writeFile('private.pem', privateKey)
    const publicKey = keyPair.publicKey.export({
        type: 'spki',
        format: 'pem'
    })
    await writeFile('public.pem', publicKey)
})()
```

The preceding code generates a new RSA key pair, containing both private and public keys, and saves them in the private.pem and public.pem files, respectively.

As in most other code samples we've seen so far, we begin by importing the three modules we need: crypto, fs, and util. We then "promisify" two methods so that they can be used with the await keyword. As we saw previously, our actual code is placed inside an **Immediately-Invoked Function Expression (IIFE)**, so we can use the async/await pattern.

The main part of the code is the invocation of the (async) crypto.generateKeyPair method, with two arguments. The first specifies that we want an RSA key. The second is a dictionary with options that are specific to each key type; for RSA keys, we need to set the size of the key (technically, the length of the modulus), which is usually one of **4,096**, **3,072**, or **2,048** bits.

The choice of the key length is an important one that depends on a variety of factors. First of all, keys shorter than 2,048 bits should not be used at this point as they can be brute-forced too easily with modern hardware. When you're choosing between 2,048 or 4,096 bits (or 3,072), keep in mind that while longer keys do provide better security, they also take longer to generate, use more resources during encryption/decryption, and require more storage for the keys, the encrypted data, and the digital signatures (as we'll see in *Chapter 6, Digital Signatures with Node.js and Trust*). Additionally, if you need to work with hardware tokens (such as smart cards), check their limitations, as some may not support keys longer than 2,048 bits.

A 2,048-bit key is considered comparable in strength to a 112-bit symmetric key (think of it as if you were using AES with a 112-bit key), and at the time of writing, it's acceptable for many applications; however, researchers expect that the minimum recommended key length will be increased in the next few years. Ultimately, the choice of the key size is up to you, your security needs, and whether your environment has any constraints.

Going back to the preceding code, the key pair we generated contains two properties: `keyPair.privateKey` and `keyPair.publicKey`. For each key, we export them as PEM (using the `export` method we covered in the previous section) and then write the keys to files called `private.pem` and `public.pem`, respectively.

When you run the preceding code sample, you will see the two files being created alongside your code, which can be opened and inspected.

Use OpenSSL to Generate an RSA Key Pair

If you need to generate an RSA key pair outside of Node.js, you can also use the OpenSSL utility, which is shipped by default on Linux and macOS and can be installed on Windows as well. OpenSSL offers a complete, open source toolkit for working with cryptography on the command line.

With OpenSSL, you can generate a new RSA key pair with two commands, with the same results as our Node.js code. The first generates the private key (with a 4,096-bit modulus in this case), while the second extracts the public key from the private one:

```
$ openssl genrsa -out private.pem 4096
$ openssl rsa -in private.pem -outform PEM -pubout
-out public.pem
```

Using RSA for encryption and decryption

Now that we've generated a new key pair, we can use it to encrypt and decrypt messages.

Before we dive into the code, it's important to point out that while you can use RSA to encrypt arbitrary data, it comes with some severe limitations. In particular, with a 2,048-bit key, the maximum amount of data that can be encrypted is 256 bytes, which is further reduced to just 190 bytes when we introduce the OAEP+SHA-256 padding, as we'll see in the following example.

Because of that, unless you're looking at encrypting only very short messages, in most cases, you will use RSA just to encrypt a symmetric key (such as a random 32-byte key to use with AES-256) to create a hybrid cryptosystem, just like we learned about in the introduction; we'll see code samples for doing this in the *Hybrid encryption with RSA and AES* section shortly.

To start, we can define a function to encrypt messages using RSA:

5.2: rsaEncrypt (from rsa-encrypt.js)

```
function rsaEncrypt(publicKey, plaintext) {
    return crypto.publicEncrypt(
        {
            key: publicKey,
            padding: crypto.constants.RSA_PKCS1_OAEP_PADDING,
            oaepHash: 'sha256'
        },
        plaintext
    )
}
```

This function accepts two parameters – a public key and the plaintext message to encrypt. Recall that with public-key cryptography, you always use the *public key to encrypt* data and the *private key to decrypt*.

The main part of this function is the invocation of `crypto.publicEncrypt`, which receives two arguments, with the second being the plaintext message. The first one is a dictionary with a few options:

- `key` is the public key; for example, a `crypto.KeyObject` object that's loaded with `crypto.createPublicKey`, as we saw earlier.

- `padding` determines the padding algorithm to use. Plain RSA (also called "textbook RSA") is vulnerable to a few different attacks, so padding is used to add random data to the plaintext message before it's encrypted. While it's possible to use RSA without padding (also with Node.js), that should be avoided at all costs.

There are two main padding algorithms, which are defined in Node.js as constants: `crypto.constants.RSA_PKCS1_OAEP_PADDING` (officially OAEP, or PKCS#1 v2 padding) and `crypto.constants.RSA_PKCS1_PADDING` (PKCS#1 v1.5). You should prefer OAEP in all cases whenever possible. PKCS#1 v1.5 is vulnerable to certain kinds of attacks and should only be used when strictly necessary, such as for compatibility with other systems that don't support OAEP.

- `oaepHash` determines the hashing algorithm to use when you're using OAEP padding (it's ignored when you're using PKCS#1 v1.5). By default, Node.js uses SHA-1 as the hashing algorithm (the string value is `'sha1'`), so in our code, we're specifying `'sha256'` instead as value. Although we've seen in previous chapters how SHA-1 is broken *in normal circumstances*, note that in this specific case, cryptographers don't believe using SHA-1 is *necessarily bad*, as the known attacks against SHA-1 should not be applicable in these situations. Nevertheless, unless you need to preserve compatibility with other systems that only support SHA-1 for hashing with OAEP, it may not be a bad idea to use SHA-256 in this case as well, following the trend of phasing out the older hashing algorithms entirely.

The return value of `crypto.publicEncrypt` (and conversely, the return value of our `rsaEncrypt` function) is a `Buffer` object containing the message that's been encrypted with RSA.

Conversely, to decrypt data, we can define a `rsaDecrypt` function, as follows:

5.3: rsaDecrypt (from rsa-encrypt.js)

```
function rsaDecrypt(privateKey, message) {
    return crypto.privateDecrypt(
        {
            key: privateKey,
            padding: crypto.constants.RSA_PKCS1_OAEP_PADDING,
            oaepHash: 'sha256'
        },
        message
    )
}
```

This function, which takes an encrypted `message` and returns the plaintext data in a `Buffer` object, is very similar to the previous, but has one... key difference (*pun intended*): it uses the private key rather than the public one. It uses the `crypto.privateDecrypt` method, receiving the private key (in a `crypto.KeyObject` object) as the first argument.

Using the `rsaEncrypt` and `rsaDecrypt` functions we defined previously requires loading a public and/or private key (for example, using `crypto.createPublicKey` or `crypto.createPrivateKey` to read them from a file or data that's been received over the network).

For brevity, we will not show a full example of using those functions in this chapter, but you can find the full code sample (exhaustively commented) in this book's GitHub repository, in the `ch5-asymmetric-and-hybrid-encryption/rsa-encrypt.js` file.

Hybrid encryption with RSA and AES

As we mentioned in the introduction and the previous section, public-key cryptography is rarely used to encrypt large amounts of data. Asymmetric ciphers are a lot slower than symmetric ones, both in theory (the algorithms themselves are more computationally intensive) and in the practical implementations, especially given how ciphers such as AES benefit from hardware acceleration in most modern CPUs.

In practice, applications commonly use hybrid cryptosystems, in which the data is encrypted with a symmetric cipher (using a randomly generated key), and then the key is wrapped (that is, encrypted) using a public-key cipher.

Let's look at one example of hybrid encryption/decryption using RSA and a symmetric cipher. This code snippet uses the `rsaEncrypt` and `rsaDecrypt` functions we defined previously, as well as two generic `symmetricEncrypt` and `symmetricDecrypt` functions. For the last two, you can use any function that performs encryption and decryption with a symmetric key, such as those we've seen in *Chapter 4, Symmetric Encryption in Node.js*, for using AES-GCM or ChaCha20-Poly1305 (likewise, AES-CBC is an option too in case authenticated encryption isn't required):

5.4: hybridEncrypt and hybridDecrypt (from rsa-hybrid-encrypt.js)

```
const crypto = require('crypto')
const util = require('util')
const randomBytes = util.promisify(crypto.randomBytes)


async function hybridEncrypt(publicKey, plaintext) {
    const symmetricKey = await randomBytes(32)
    const encrypted = await symmetricEncrypt(symmetricKey,
        plaintext)
    const wrappedKey = rsaEncrypt(publicKey, symmetricKey)
```

```
    return {encrypted, wrappedKey}
}


function hybridDecrypt(privateKey, wrappedKey, message) {
    const symmetricKey = rsaDecrypt(privateKey, wrappedKey)
    const decrypted = symmetricDecrypt(symmetricKey, message)
    return decrypted.toString('utf8')
}
```

Let's look at this code in detail while highlighting the differences between the previous
rsaEncrypt and rsaDecrypt functions:

1. The hybridEncrypt function begins by generating a random sequence of bytes
    (using a "promisified" crypto.randomBytes function), which will be used as
    a symmetric key. The length of the byte sequence depends on the algorithm that's
    used; in our case, we're using 32 bytes, as is required by AES-256.

2. The function then invokes a generic symmetricEncrypt function (as we saw
    previously, this could, for example, be a function that performs encryption with
    AES-256-GCM) that uses the random byte sequence as the encryption key.

3. Next, hybridEncrypt uses RSA to wrap the symmetric key using the public
    key (remember that we use public keys to encrypt data). This uses the same
    rsaEncrypt function we defined earlier and used to encrypt arbitrary data, except
    that this time, the "arbitrary data" is the symmetric key we generated in *Step 1*.

4. Lastly, hybridEncrypt returns an object with two values: the encrypted message
    (encrypted using the symmetric key) and the wrapped key (encrypted using RSA).
    A consumer application will need both to be able to successfully decrypt the data.

5. Similarly, hybridDecrypt performs the operations in the opposite order. It starts
    by using the private key to unwrap (decrypt) the symmetric key (again, remember
    we use a private key to decrypt data). The result should be the same symmetric key
    that we randomly generated inside hybridEncrypt.

6. hybridDecrypt then uses the symmetric key to decrypt the message, invoking
    a generic symmetricDecrypt function (which should use the same algorithm as
    what symmetricEncrypt used previously). The function returns the plaintext as
    a UTF-8 string.

To use these functions, we can write some code similar to this:

5.5: Using hybridEncrypt and hybridDecrypt (from rsa-hybrid-encrypt.js)

```js
const crypto = require('crypto')
const fs = require('fs')
const util = require('util')
const readFile = util.promisify(fs.readFile)

;(async function() {
    const plaintext = 'Hello world!'
    const publicKeyObject = crypto.createPublicKey(
        await readFile('public.pem')
    )
    const privateKeyObject = crypto.createPrivateKey(
        await readFile('private.pem')
    )
    const {encrypted, wrappedKey} = await
        hybridEncrypt(publicKeyObject, plaintext)
    console.log('Encrypted message and wrapped key', {
        encrypted: encrypted.toString('base64'),
        wrappedKey: wrappedKey.toString('base64'),
    })
    const decrypted = hybridDecrypt(privateKeyObject,
        wrappedKey, encrypted)
    console.log('Decrypted message:', decrypted.
        toString('utf8'))
})()
```

Inside the main part of the code, we start by loading the public and private keys from files, as we did earlier.

Next, we invoke hybridEncrypt with the public key and the plaintext, receiving the encrypted message and the wrapped symmetric key in return.

Those last two values (the wrapped key and the encrypted message), together with the private key, are then passed to hybridDecrypt, which returns the original plaintext message.

Before we end this section, it's important to note that there's no standard for hybrid encryption: this is more of a practice (or pattern) than a formal specification. Because of that, when you're designing a hybrid cryptosystem that is meant to be used to communicate with other applications, you need to ensure that every participant agrees on the algorithms used, the key sizes, the modes of operations, and so on.

With this, we've concluded our exploration of using RSA as an asymmetric cipher to encrypt and decrypt data. We'll pick up RSA again in *Chapter 6, Digital Signatures with Node.js and Trust*, this time writing about digital signatures, but first we shall look at using ECC as an alternative to RSA for encrypting data.

Key agreements with Elliptic-Curve Diffie-Hellman

Over the last few years, **ECC** has been gaining momentum as an alternative to RSA, being used in an ever-increasing number of applications and scenarios.

While RSA is considered a safe and reliable algorithm (assuming a long-enough key size is chosen and the proper precautions, such as the correct use of padding, are in place) and having been first published in 1977 it certainly falls into the category of "tried and tested" cryptosystems, there are certain advantages to ECC that make it appealing.

Algorithms based on **Elliptic Curves** (**EC**) are generally faster and use fewer resources, thus being more desirable on smaller, less powerful systems (such as IoT devices). Additionally, ECs offer the same level of security as RSA while using significantly smaller keys: a 256-bit EC key is comparable in strength to a 3,072-bit RSA key. Not only are smaller keys easier to manage, but they also produce smaller signatures (as we'll see in the next chapter, *Chapter 6, Digital Signatures with Node.js and Trust*).

Unlike RSA, ECC cannot be used for encrypting and decrypting data. However, it's possible to use ECs in hybrid encryption schemes with a key agreement algorithm called **Elliptic-Curve Diffie-Hellman**, or **ECDH**.

Picking a curve

Before we start, we need to pick which curve to use. As if ECC wasn't hard enough to deal with, given the amount of complex math that is behind that, we can choose from a very large number of curves, with strange and confusing names.

In fact, inside Node.js, you can use the `crypto.getCurves` function to get a list of all the ECs that are available in your system; on the machine that I'm currently using, the resulting array has 82 elements (this number will vary depending on the version of Node.js you're using and the version of the OpenSSL library it's linked to).

Not all ECs are made equal, and despite the vast choice, there are only two curves that you may want to choose from:

- The first one is **P-256**, which is called `prime256v1` in Node.js and sometimes referred to as `secp256r1`. Because P-256 is defined in the NIST standard, this curve is currently the most widely used on the Internet among all ECs (most browsers use it for the TLS key exchange as well) and enjoys the broadest support in software and even hardware, such as security keys.

- The second is **Curve25519**, which (to make things even more confusing) is implemented as **X25519** in the context of ECDH, and as **Ed25519** for digital signatures (as we'll see in *Chapter 6, Digital Signatures with Node.js and Trust*). Developed by Daniel J. Bernstein, the same cryptographer who created ChaCha20-Poly1305, this is a newer curve that is growing fast in popularity: it is included as an option in the TLS 1.3 standard, and it's already supported by various applications, web browsers, services, and CDNs. Recently, the NIST has approved the use of X25519 too.

Both curves offer the same level of security and have comparable speed (at least at the level humans can perceive; X25519 should be faster than P-256 for ECDH, but the difference is negligible in practical terms). P-256 largely wins in terms of support across the widest number of systems.

The main reason why several cryptographers are pushing for Curve25519 is connected to the origins of P-256 at the NIST. To keep it short, P-256 relies on parameters that were chosen by its designers in a seemingly arbitrary way, which the NIST hasn't been able to explain clearly. This has led to people wondering if the choice was influenced by the NSA to introduce a "backdoor" in the curve, with a move that would allow the agency to break cryptography based on P-256 in ways that are known only to them. At the time of writing this book, no evidence in support of these allegations has been found, and all of this amounts to little more than a "conspiracy theory." Regardless, supported by many cryptographers' mistrust in the NSA, the **FUD (Fear, Uncertainty, and Doubt)** around P-256's origins has been good marketing for Curve25519, driving a fast increase in adoption.

> **Honorable Mention: secp256k1**
>
> Among the vast number of other ECs that are available, it's worth mentioning secp256k1 too, as this is a core part of Bitcoin. Not to be confused with secp256r1 (an alias for P-256), it's a different kind of curve that offers comparable, but slightly lesser, security. It's unclear why Satoshi Nakamoto, the mysterious author of Bitcoin, opted for this curve, which does not have a lot of usage outside of cryptocurrencies.

Generating EC key pairs

To start, let's look at how we can generate EC key pairs with Node.js using the `crypto` module. To do that, we can use the same `crypto.generateKeyPair(type, [options])` function that we used to compute RSA key pairs, with slightly different parameters.

Please note that all these samples assume that `crypto.generateKeyPair` has been "promisified" with the following code:

```
const {promisify} = require('util')
const generateKeyPair = promisify(crypto.generateKeyPair)
```

Most types of EC key pairs are generated by passing `'ec'` as the `type` argument, then passing `options` as a dictionary that contains the name of the curve in the `namedCurve` property. For example, to generate a **prime256v1 (P-256)** curve, we can use the following code:

```
const keyPair = await generateKeyPair('ec', {
    namedCurve: 'prime256v1'
})
```

There are two exceptions to this format, with one being **Curve25519**. For generating key pairs for Curve25519, set the `type` argument to `'x25519'` if the key is to be used for ECDH (as in this chapter), or `'ed25519'` if the key is for digital signatures (as we'll see in *Chapter 6, Digital Signatures with Node.js and Trust*):

```
const keyPairForECDH = await generateKeyPair('x25519')
const keyPairForSig = await generateKeyPair('ed25519')
```

Just like when we generated RSA key pairs, the returned value of the `crypto.generateKeyPair` method is an object that contains both the `privateKey` and `publicKey` properties. And, just like with RSA keys, those can be exported with the `export` method – except that you cannot use `'pkcs1'` as the value for the type option (the PKCS#1 standard is defined for RSA keys only).

Generating EC key Pairs with OpenSSL

We can use OpenSSL to generate EC key pairs too but note that this requires a recent version of OpenSSL (1.1.0 or higher). To generate P-256 private keys, use the following code:

```
$ openssl genpkey -algorithm ec -pkeyopt
ec_paramgen_curve:prime256v1 -out private.pem
```

For an X25519 or Ed25519 private key, use one of the following, respectively:

```
$ openssl genpkey -algorithm x25519 -out private.
pem
```

```
$ openssl genpkey -algorithm ed25519 -out private.
pem
```

In both these cases, you can then extract the public key with the following command:

```
$ openssl pkey -in private.pem -pubout -out
public.pem
```

Diffie-Hellman key agreements and Perfect Forward Secrecy

Before we dive deep into ECDH, we need to understand how key agreement protocols such as **Diffie-Hellman (DH)** work and how they enable hybrid cryptosystems.

The DH algorithm, named after its inventors Whitfield Diffie and Martin Hellman, has been around since 1976 (in fact, it predates RSA by one year); in this book, we'll use the **ECDH variant**, a more recent one that is based on ECs and offers increased protection against certain attacks such as Logjam, which was publicly reported in 2015.

The entire point of all key exchange protocols is to securely transmit a symmetric encryption key over an insecure channel. We have been talking about this as the domain of public-key cryptography since the very beginning of this chapter. However, there are multiple ways to accomplish this.

In the previous section, we implemented a key exchange using RSA. Bringing back cryptographers' best friends Alice and Bob, in that case, Alice used Bob's public key to encrypt the symmetric key (which was randomly generated), then submitted the wrapped key to Bob along with the ciphertext.

On the other hand, DH algorithms (including ECDH) allow us to perform a key agreement as a special kind of key exchange. In this case, Alice and Bob have a way to agree on a **shared secret**, which each of them can compute independently just by knowing the other person's public key. Entirely glossing over the mathematical explanation, we will limit ourselves to describing the effects of the DH algorithms.

With an underlying agreement on a set of parameters (in the case of DH) or on an elliptic curve (in the case of ECDH), Alice and Bob generate a new key pair for every new exchange. Both share their public key with the other person and then can use the DH (or ECDH) algorithm to independently derive the same secret byte sequence: this is what is used as the symmetric encryption key.

The differences between a DH key agreement and a key exchange using an algorithm such as RSA are subtle, and the net effect is identical as both parties can share a symmetric key securely over an untrusted channel. However, we can find two main differences in the way the algorithms operate, conceptually:

1. With a key exchange based on RSA, there is an external symmetric key that gets wrapped and *predates the key exchange*. This symmetric key is usually randomly generated on the spot, but it could be derived in any other way, such as from a passphrase.

    In the case of a DH key agreement, the key is generated by the two parties *as a consequence of the key exchange*.

2. When Alice sends a message to Bob with a key exchange based on RSA, Alice needs to obtain Bob's public key beforehand, then transmit the wrapped symmetric key to Bob (possibly alongside an encrypted message). Bob does not need Alice's public key – in fact, Alice may not even have her own RSA key pair. *(Note: this is specifically limited to the key encryption/exchange part and does not cover the case when Alice may also sign her message, as we'll see in the next chapter.)*

    When it comes to performing a key agreement using a DH algorithm, both Alice and Bob need each other's public keys. If Alice sends a message to Bob, she first needs to obtain Bob's public key (just like in the case of RSA), and then sends her public key to Bob (with the encrypted message if needed).

However, the most important consequence of performing a key agreement with a DH algorithm rather than using RSA is that during a DH (or ECDH) exchange, both Alice's and Bob's private keys are *ephemeral*. This means that they last only for the (usually very short) amount of time they're needed.

As you may have noticed while running the code presented previously to generate a new RSA key (or while doing that with OpenSSL), computing an RSA key pair takes a non-insignificant amount of time, especially with longer keys, such as 4,096-bit ones. Because of that, each person doing the exchange has a key pair that is reused in every exchange. As we saw earlier, with solutions such as GPG, for example, the same key pair is designed to be used for many years, and the person's public key is published on registries for everyone to see and use.

Instead, generating private keys for a DH exchange (including calculating EC key pairs for ECDH) is instantaneous, so each party presents a new, ephemeral key each time.

This allows for an interesting benefit called **Perfect Forward Secrecy** (**PFS**), which is defined as the ability to protect past sessions against future compromises of a key.

Suppose that an attacker can intercept the encrypted data being exchanged by two parties: without knowledge of the key that was used to encrypt it, the attacker would not be able to look at the plaintext. However, without PFS, if the attacker were able to exfiltrate the key in the future (for example, by compromising a person's laptop), they would be able to retroactively decrypt every message that was sent to that person in the past, from anyone.

Instead, when the keys are ephemeral, as in the case of a DH (or ECDH) key agreement, we can achieve PFS: a compromise of a single key would allow an attacker to compromise that session only.

For example, imagine the situation of a web server using TLS (the algorithm that makes HTTPS possible) which performed key exchanges with an algorithm that didn't offer PFS. An attacker that steals the server's private key would be able to retroactively decrypt all the traffic that's sent and received by that server in the past – so, every single web page that every client requested. Thankfully, modern TLS performs key exchanges with DH algorithms: each client uses a different session, each one with keys that are periodically rotated, thus achieving PFS.

Performing an ECDH key agreement

Finally, let's look at how to use ECDH to perform a key agreement in this first example:

5.6: Key agreement with ECDH (ecdh.js)

```
const crypto = require('crypto')
const {promisify} = require('util')
const generateKeyPair = promisify(crypto.generateKeyPair)

;(async function() {
```

```
const aliceKeyPair = await generateKeyPair('ec', {
    namedCurve: 'prime256v1'
})
const alicePublicKeyPem = aliceKeyPair.publicKey.export(
    {type: 'spki', format: 'pem'}
)
const bobKeyPair = await generateKeyPair('ec', {
    namedCurve: 'prime256v1'
})
const bobPublicKeyPem = bobKeyPair.publicKey.export(
    {type: 'spki', format: 'pem'}
)
const aliceSharedSecret = crypto.diffieHellman({
    publicKey: crypto.createPublicKey(bobPublicKeyPem),
    privateKey: aliceKeyPair.privateKey
})
const bobSharedSecret = crypto.diffieHellman({
    publicKey: crypto.createPublicKey(alicePublicKeyPem),
    privateKey: bobKeyPair.privateKey
})
console.log(aliceSharedSecret.toString('hex'))
console.log(bobSharedSecret.toString('hex'))
})()
```

This example, which is almost "trivial" in the fact that the key "exchange" happens within the same function, demonstrates the various operations that are required to perform an ECDH key agreement and generate a shared secret:

1. To start, we generate a new key pair for both Alice and Bob. Generating EC keys is instant, so we can create new, ephemeral key pairs for each exchange, and achieve PFS as explained in the previous section. The key pairs are stored in the aliceKeyPair and bobKeyPair objects.

2. We also export both public keys, encoding them as PEM and keeping them in the alicePublicKeyPem and bobPublicKeyPem variables.

3. We then assume that Bob sent Alice his public key, so Alice can calculate the shared secret on her own. Using crypto.diffieHellman, Alice calculates aliceSharedSecret using her private key and Bob's public key (the latter is converted back into a crypto.KeyObject object using crypto.createPublicKey, as we saw earlier).

4. On Bob's side, he performs the same operation to compute `bobSharedSecret` on his own but using his private key and Alice's public key. This is the opposite of what Alice did: each person uses their *private* key and the other person's *public* key.

5. At the end of the function, we print out `aliceSharedSecret` and `bobSharedSecret` (they're both `Buffer` objects, so we hex-encode them first). While they'll be different each time because they're generated from random key pairs, both variables will contain the identical shared secret.

While the previous code sample demonstrates all the steps that are required to perform an ECDH exchange, I recognize that because it's "compressed" into a single function, it doesn't clearly show the flow of information between Alice and Bob: how they transmit their public keys to each other.

In this book's GitHub repository, you can find a more comprehensive example that demonstrates performing an ECDH exchange between a client and server: in the `ch5-asymmetric-and-hybrid-encryption` folder, look for the `ecdh-server.js` and `ecdh-client.js` files. To run that sample, first, start the sample server in the `ecdh-server.js` file, and then use `ecdh-client.js` to make requests and generate new shared secrets that are printed in the terminal. Both files are extensively commented to explain the various parts of the code.

Data encryption with ECIES

At this point, after having understood how we can use ECDH to perform a key agreement between two parties using ECC, the logical next step is to use the shared key to encrypt and decrypt data.

The scheme that's used in this scenario is called **Elliptic Curve Integrated Encryption Scheme (ECIES)**, which is a hybrid one based on ECC.

With ECIES, there isn't a single, universally agreed-upon specification that describes how to implement it. There are at least four standards that specify how to implement ECIES, usually in broad terms and in some cases conflicting with the other standards. All specifications, however, require four things to use ECIES correctly:

1. A **Key Agreement (KA)** function, which is used to establish a shared secret. In our case, that will be ECDH.

2. A **Key Derivation Function (KDF)**. Because the shared secret that's generated by ECDH isn't uniformly random, it's not suitable to be used as a symmetric key as-is; instead, it's a best practice to stretch it with a KDF and a random salt. As we saw in *Chapter 3, File and Password Hashing with Node.js*, a KDF is just a hashing function whose output is suitable to be used as an encryption key.

In this case, we're going to use a salted SHA-256 hash as our KDF. That is, our symmetric encryption key will be the SHA-256 hash of the concatenation of the shared secret and a random 16-byte salt.

3. A **symmetric encryption algorithm** – in this case, we'll be using AES-256-GCM.

4. Lastly, we need a **Message Authentication Code** (**MAC**), which is a special kind of hash that's used to authenticate the integrity of a message. In our case, we won't need to perform anything special for this: because we're using AES-GCM, which is an authenticated cipher, we are automatically getting an authentication tag, which is a MAC.

Using SHA-256 as a KDF

You may be wondering why we're using SHA-256 as a KDF, given how much emphasis we put in *Chapter 3, File and Password Hashing with Node.js*, on how straight hashing functions are not suitable for key derivation. If you think that we're going against our previous advice in this chapter, you're not wrong.

In this specific case, however, we are not generating a key from a passphrase (which is a low-entropy input), but rather from a shared secret that is already a "random" sequence of bytes. By adding a random salt, we're providing enough entropy so that a straight hashing function can be used as a KDF safely in this case.

Just like we discussed earlier in the context of hybrid encryption schemes built around RSA, because there isn't a precise standard for using ECIES, you need to document and share the choices you've made around algorithms, key sizes, modes of operation, and so on. This will enable your app to communicate with others effectively.

Let's look at some example code for implementing ECIES using the choices we made previously. Assuming that Alice wants to send a message to Bob using the algorithms defined previously, we can define the function that Alice uses to encrypt the data (which we'll call `AliceEncrypt` in this example) and the one that Bob uses to decrypt the data (`BobDecrypt`).

Please note that the following code depends on generic `aesEncrypt` and `aesDecrypt` functions for using AES-256-GCM, such as those that we defined in *Chapter 4, Symmetric Encryption in Node.js*:

5.7: Encryption and decryption with ECIES (part of ecies.js)

```
const crypto = require('crypto')
const randomBytes = require('util').promisify(crypto.
    randomBytes)
```

```
async function AliceEncrypt(alicePrivateKey, bobPublicKey,
    message) {
  const sharedSecret = crypto.diffieHellman({
    publicKey: bobPublicKey,
    privateKey: alicePrivateKey
  })
  const salt = await randomBytes(16)
  const symmetricKey = crypto.createHash('sha256')
    .update(Buffer.concat([sharedSecret, salt]))
    .digest()
  const encryptedMessage = await aesEncrypt(symmetricKey,
    message)
  return Buffer.concat([salt, encryptedMessage])
}
```

```
function BobDecrypt(bobPrivateKey, alicePublicKey,
    encryptedMessage) {
  const sharedSecret = crypto.diffieHellman({
    publicKey: alicePublicKey,
    privateKey: bobPrivateKey
  })
  const salt = encryptedMessage.slice(0, 16)
  const symmetricKey = crypto.createHash('sha256')
    .update(Buffer.concat([sharedSecret, salt]))
    .digest()
  return aesDecrypt(symmetricKey, encryptedMessage.slice(16))
}
```

The function Alice uses to encrypt a message requires three arguments: Alice's private key, Bob's public key, and the message to encrypt. This is just like in the previous section in which we covered ECDH, each person computes the shared secret using their private key and the other person's public key.

The AliceEncrypt function begins by computing the shared secret (just like we did in the *Performing an ECDH key agreement* section), then derives a symmetric encryption key. As we saw in the description of the algorithm, the symmetric key is calculated as the SHA-256 hash of the concatenation of the shared secret with a random 16-byte salt.

The message is then encrypted with AES-256-GCM, using a function like the one we defined in the previous chapter. Finally, `AliceEncrypt` returns a `Buffer` object with the concatenation of the random salt (used in the KDF) and the encrypted message (which also includes the authentication tag).

Conversely, `BobDecrypt` performs the same operations in reverse order. It accepts three arguments: Bob's private key, Alice's public key, and the encrypted message, as returned by `AliceEncrypt` (with the salt for the KDF at the beginning).

The decryption function begins by computing the shared secret again, using Bob's private key and Alice's public key. Then, it extracts the salt from the beginning of the encrypted message and uses that to calculate the symmetric key exactly as Alice did. With that key and the rest of the encrypted message, it invokes the function that's performing decryption with AES-256-GCM. Lastly, `BobDecrypt` returns the original message as plaintext.

To use `AliceEncrypt` and `BobDecrypt`, we can simulate an exchange in a single function (just like we did in the previous ECDH example):

5.8: Using the ECIES functions to encrypt and decrypt a message (part of ecies.js)

```
const crypto = require('crypto')
const {promisify} = require('util')
const generateKeyPair = promisify(crypto.generateKeyPair)


;(async function() {
    const message = 'Hello world'
    const aliceKeyPair = await generateKeyPair('x25519')
    const alicePublicKeyPem = aliceKeyPair.publicKey.export({
        type: 'spki',
        format: 'pem'
    })
    const bobKeyPair = await generateKeyPair('x25519')
    const bobPublicKeyPem = bobKeyPair.publicKey.export({
        type: 'spki',
        format: 'pem'
```

```
    })
    const encrypted = await AliceEncrypt(
        aliceKeyPair.privateKey,
        crypto.createPublicKey(bobPublicKeyPem),
        message
    )
    const decrypted = BobDecrypt(
        bobKeyPair.privateKey,
        crypto.createPublicKey(alicePublicKeyPem),
        encrypted
    )
    console.log('The decrypted message is:', decrypted)
})()
```

The code within the IIFE starts by generating a key pair for both Alice and Bob, just like in the ECDH code we saw earlier (this time, we're using keys of the x25519 type to offer a different example). It invokes AliceEncrypt to encrypt the message, and then BobDecrypt to decrypt it again. After running this code, you should see that the decrypted message in the console is Hello world.

Once again, in this book's GitHub repository, you can find a more complete example of performing encryption and decryption with ECIES between a server and a client. While the cryptography that's used will be identical to the one in the preceding code sample, having two separate apps communicating with each offers a more real-world example of how ECIES can be used.

In this book's GitHub repository, in the ch5-asymmetric-and-hybrid-encryption folder, look for the ecies-server.js and ecies-client.js files. To run those, first, start the sample server in the ecies-server.js file (with the node ecies-server.js command, leaving the terminal running), and then use ecies-client.js (with the node ecies-client.js command in a different terminal) to make requests and see how the server's console outputs the messages in plaintext. Both files contain comments explaining the code in detail.

Summary

In this chapter, we focused on asymmetric and hybrid cryptosystems, learning about the kinds of problems that they help solve.

On the practical side, we learned about managing public and private keys within a Node.js application. We then implemented encryption and decryption using RSA, both standalone and in a hybrid system with AES. Lastly, we learned about key agreements with Diffie-Hellman algorithms, specifically the ECDH variant, which is based on ECC, and we used them to perform hybrid encryption with ECIES.

In the next chapter, we'll look at another very common use of public-key cryptography, which is digital signatures. We'll understand their purpose and how we can calculate and verify them in a Node.js application.

6
Digital Signatures with Node.js and Trust

In the previous chapter, we learned about asymmetric cryptography, also called public-key cryptography because it relies on pairs of public/private keys, and we used that to encrypt messages.

In this chapter, we'll begin by looking at public key cryptography's other main use, which is calculating digital signatures. When attached to a message (encrypted or not), these offer a guarantee that the content is intact and that the sender is indeed the person they're claiming to be. Digital signatures are the last class of cryptographic operations we'll be analyzing in this book.

Before we end this chapter, we'll also learn how to deal with the problem of trusting public keys. We'll look at some techniques that are commonly used to bind keys to a real identity, such as an individual or an organization, and why that matters.

In this chapter, we're going to cover the following main topics:

- Understanding digital signatures – what they are, how they're generated, and the role they play in cryptography and the real world.

- How to generate digital signatures with Node.js, using RSA and **Elliptic-Curve Cryptography** (**ECC**) (specifically, ECDSA with the P-256 curve and EdDSA with the Ed25519 curve).

- The problem of trusting keys and binding a key to a real-world identity and how certificates are used in this space. We'll also introduce the ideas of **Public Key Infrastructure** (**PKI**) and some alternative approaches.

Technical requirements

All the code samples for this chapter can be found in this book's GitHub repository at `https://bit.ly/crypto-ch6`.

The what, how, and why of digital signatures

When we covered hashing in *Chapter 3, File and Password Hashing with Node.js*, we mentioned that we were going to be leveraging hashing functions in virtually every part of this book, and as we're looking at the last class of operations – digital signatures – we're certainly staying true to our word once again. In a sense, we could even say that digital signatures are an extension of hashes!

Hashes and digital signatures

Let's start with an example: you are sending a message to your bank, asking them "*Please wire $100 to Alice.*" You want to be sure that the message doesn't get corrupted in transit (the difference between "$100" and "$500" is just one flipped bit!), so you attach a hash of the message. As we saw in *Chapter 3, File and Password Hashing with Node.js*, one of the main purposes of hashes is to guarantee the integrity of a message: a change in even a single bit would produce a different checksum.

However, while hashes offer a guarantee of integrity, they alone do not offer protection against tampering, especially when they are sent alongside the message. In the preceding example, an attacker (in this case, called a **Man-in-the-Middle** or **MitM** – an industry term that should arguably be updated to a more inclusive one) could intercept your message, change the name of the recipient to Mallory (*a name often used by cryptographers, just like Alice and Bob, to refer to malicious attackers*), re-compute the hash, and update the one contained in the message.

The message you originally sent and its SHA-256 hash are as follows:

Please wire $100 to Alice
27b536f40b7d2d6e70acd2273df7a832942eb3363bf3cfde2117dbfb6be1aaea

But the attacker changes your message and its hash to the following:

Please wire $100 to Mallory
e9fb35ae3ee0441bde2edbbcc7f02a7c12d5ba989c6aba25bc5e52bd3e484758

When your bank receives the hijacked message, they can confirm its integrity because the checksum is correct, yet they have no way to know that Mallory changed the content! This is because hashes guarantee integrity, but they do not authenticate the message.

At their core, digital signatures are a solution to this problem: they allow you to append a signature that is based on a hash, but which uses public-key cryptography to offer additional protection against tampering.

Properties of digital signatures

All digital signatures offer three properties:

- **Integrity**: Because they're based on hashes, they offer protection against manipulation or corruption of the message while in transit.

- **Authentication**: Thanks to the usage of public-key cryptography, they offer a guarantee that the person who signed the message is really who they say they are.

- **Non-repudiation**: The person who signed the message cannot dispute that they were the actual creator of the message. That is, a person cannot later deny that they were the one signing the message.

Digital signatures are based on public-key cryptography, and as long as a person's private key is not compromised, all these three properties remain true.

Going back to our previous example, if instead of a simple hash we had attached a digital signature to our message, Mallory would not have been able to change the message and get away with it. Assuming that they don't have your private key, Mallory can't generate another digital signature appearing as yours (that is, signed with your key). This is an example of how digital signatures offer integrity (Mallory can't change the message without making the signature check fail) and authentication (Mallory could create a new signature using their key, but then the bank would see that the key that was used was Mallory's and not yours).

Lastly, because signatures are non-repudiable, if you changed your mind about sending money to Alice, you wouldn't be able to call your bank and lie about someone else having sent the message.

How digital signatures work

As usual, in this book, we won't get into the details of how the algorithms work – that is, how they're implemented. At a high level, all digital signature schemes work by using a private key to "encrypt" the checksum of our message. Other people can then verify the digital signature by using your public key to "decrypt" the checksum of the message and verify that it matches what they calculated.

There are two important things to highlight here:

- Digital signatures are based on hashes. When you compute a signature, you need to calculate the checksum of the message first. Likewise, when you verify a signature, you compare the checksum that is contained in the signature with the one you compute on the message you received.

- Digital signatures are calculated using asymmetric cryptography, but the role of each key is inverted.

  For data encryption (as we saw in *Chapter 5, Using Asymmetric and Hybrid Encryption in Node.js*), you use the public key to encrypt a message and the private key to decrypt it.

  For digital signatures, it's the opposite: the signature is **computed with the private key** and it's **verified with the public key**.

The last part is perhaps the most confusing aspect, but you can make sense of that by remembering that the public key is what is meant to be shared with the world, while the private key must be kept confidential. Our objective is to allow others to verify that the signatures we add to our messages are valid, and the only way for them to do that is to use our public key.

Signatures are always attached to (or, in general, shared alongside with) the original message. Because the signature doesn't contain the message, but only its hash, to verify a signature a person needs to have the original, plaintext message too.

As a corollary to the last sentence, there's no need for signatures to be kept secret: with a signature alone, it's impossible to retrieve the original message, just like you can't retrieve the original message from its hash as we saw in *Chapter 3, File and Password Hashing with Node.js*.

Digital signatures and encryption

Digital signatures are often used together with public-key encryption schemes too, as they complement each other nicely.

Encrypting data provides confidentiality. Going back once more to the previous example in which we sent a message to our bank, we could use the bank's public key to encrypt the message to ensure that no one else but the bank employees can read it, using the bank's private key. On top of that, digital signatures guarantee integrity, authentication, and non-repudiation. This signature is calculated using your private key, and the bank can verify it using your public key. Of course, this means that both you and the bank need to know the other party's public key.

Many applications that are used to encrypt data using public-key algorithms automatically include signatures too, such as GPG.

Signatures are generally computed on the plaintext message. Even when the message is confidential and shared in encrypted form, it's OK for the signature to be shared along with the ciphertext, as it does not need to be kept secret.

How developers use digital signatures

While digital signatures are perhaps among the least widely known (or understood) of the various cryptographic operations we've seen in this book, they are nonetheless incredibly important, and they underpin a lot of the technology we use every day.

The example we looked at previously, which involves sending a signed message (such as an email), is the most immediate one. Applications such as GPG have been used for many decades to add digital signatures to messages, and optionally encrypt them too.

In one-to-one communications, it's common to use signatures together with encrypted messages, but much more frequently, signatures are being used to authenticate public messages too. In this case, a lot of people (sometimes, the entire world) can read the message, and the digital signature allows them to verify its integrity and authenticate that you wrote that.

For example, the Git version control system allows developers to add a digital signature to their commits, using GPG under the hood. When authoring a Git commit, everyone can claim to be whoever they want to be, just by setting arbitrary values for the user.name and user.email configuration options. Using GPG, developers can attach a signature to a commit to prove that they own the key associated with that name and email address. If you're interested in this topic, you can read more about how to configure commit signing on a blog post I wrote: https://withblue.ink/go/git-sign.

Blockchains use digital signatures extensively too, and in a very public fashion. When you want to send some amount of digital currency to another person, you submit a transaction request to the blockchain network that is signed with your private key, providing both authentication and non-repudiation for that transaction.

All the examples we've seen so far involve using your key to create digital signatures. In many cases, however, the signature is generated by a third party to add some level of attestation.

For example, mobile operating systems (such as iOS or Android) require all apps to be installed from app stores, and they achieve that by forcing them to have a digital signature created using the app store's key. For example, when you submit an app to the iOS App Store, Apple uses its key to calculate a digital signature of your app, sort of giving it a seal of approval. Inside iOS, Apple deployed a copy of their public key, and the operating system uses that to verify the signature and decide if an app can be executed or not.

The same technique is commonly deployed for software updates of all major operating systems. Windows and macOS updates are signed with the vendors' keys. On Linux, most distributions either use packages that are individually signed (such as RPM) or packages whose checksums are included in a signed index (such as DEB), using keys that are owned by the maintainers of that distribution only. In all these cases, digital signatures offer a very important layer of protection against attackers trying to distribute malware alongside system packages, such as by breaking into the update servers or performing MitM attacks.

Lastly, perhaps the most important use of digital signatures is with certificates, which are used by a **Certificate Authority** (**CA**) to authenticate public keys. This is part of the **Public Key Infrastructure** (**PKI**), which underpins TLS and protocols based on that (such as HTTPS); we'll talk more about that in the second part of this chapter, in the *Trust and certificates section*.

> **Guaranteeing Time**
>
> Tangentially related to this topic, it may be worth highlighting that digital signatures do not offer any guarantee on the time something was signed at. This has some major implications when you're trying to use digital signatures as evidence in a court, for example.
>
> Establishing proof of time usually requires relying on a trusted third party, such as services that provide a timestamp. Those services (also called **time stamping authorities**) extend your message's checksum with the current date and time, then use their keys to digitally sign that. Alternative approaches, including blockchain-based ones, are being evaluated too.

Now that we've learned about what digital signatures are, how they work, and what we can use them for, it's finally time to look at how to generate and verify them in Node.js.

Calculating and verifying digital signatures with Node.js

In this section, we'll learn how to use Node.js to compute and verify digital signatures using RSA and ECC. Luckily for us, the Node.js built-in `crypto` module contains all the functions we need to do that.

Using RSA

To start, we're going to look at using RSA to calculate and verify digital signatures with Node.js by using `crypto.sign` and `crypto.verify`:

6.1: rsaSign and rsaVerify (part of signatures-rsa.js)

```javascript
const crypto = require('crypto')

function rsaSign(privateKey, message) {
    return crypto.sign(
        'sha256',
        message,
        {
            key: privateKey,
            padding: crypto.constants.RSA_PKCS1_PSS_PADDING
        }
    )
}

function rsaVerify(publicKey, message, signature) {
    return crypto.verify(
        'sha256',
        message,
        {
            key: publicKey,
            padding: crypto.constants.RSA_PKCS1_PSS_PADDING
        },
        signature
    )
}
```

The `rsaSign` function accepts a private key (a `crypto.KeyObject` object containing a private key) and a message, and returns the digital signature of that message, which is calculated using RSA. This function is essentially a wrapper around `crypto.sign(algorithm, data, key)` that uses the following parameters:

- For `crypto.sign`, the `algorithm` parameter defines the hashing algorithm to use. With RSA, we can sign any kind of hash, but SHA-256 (with the `'sha256'` identifier) is arguably the most appropriate choice – unless you need to use an older algorithm for compatibility with other systems that require that. For a discussion around hashing algorithms, you can go back to *Chapter 3, File and Password Hashing with Node.js.*

- The `data` parameter is the plaintext message that needs to be signed: in this case, the `message` argument that's received by `rsaSign`. This can be either a string or a `Buffer` object.

- For the third parameter, `key`, we need to pass an object containing the private key, as well as the padding we wish to use for the RSA signature.

Just like we saw in the previous chapter with regards to padding algorithms that are used for encryption with RSA, we have two different options when it comes to choosing a padding algorithm for calculating RSA digital signatures too:

- PKCS#1 v1.5, which can be used by passing the `crypto.constants.RSA_PKCS1_PADDING` constant to the `padding` key in the dictionary (and which is the default option if no value is specified).

- PSS, which in Node.js requires setting the padding key in the dictionary to `crypto.constants.RSA_PKCS1_PSS_PADDING`.

RSA-PSS is a newer padding algorithm that's defined in PKCS#1 v2.1 and improves on the previous algorithm by being non-deterministic. However, while the PKCS#1 v1.5 padding is considered broken when using RSA for encryption (as we saw in the previous chapter), it is still valid when you're using RSA for signing. Ultimately, assuming you don't need to make a choice based on compatibility requirements with external systems, either padding scheme should be acceptable.

The `rsaVerify` function, on the other hand, verifies if a signature that's been calculated with RSA (and SHA-256 as hashing) is valid for the message. This function accepts three arguments – `publicKey` (a `crypto.KeyObject` object containing the public key), `message` (the original, plaintext message that was signed and which the signature must be verified against), and `signature` (a `Buffer` object containing the signature to verify).

In the implementation of `rsaVerify`, you can see that we've used the `crypto.verify` function in a way that mirrors what we've used to calculate the signature. We need to provide the function with the same options that were used to generate the signature (the hashing algorithm and the type of padding that's used for RSA), with the only difference being that the key is a public one in this case.

To use these functions, we can invoke them with code similar to this:

6.2: Using rsaSign and rsaVerify (part of signatures-rsa.js)

```
const crypto = require('crypto')
const fs = require('fs')


const message = 'I owe Clare $100'
const privateKeyObject = crypto.createPrivateKey(
    fs.readFileSync('private.pem')
)
const signature = rsaSign(privateKeyObject, message)
console.log('Message:', message)
console.log('Signature:', signature.toString('base64'))
const publicKeyObject = crypto.createPublicKey(
    fs.readFileSync('public.pem')
)
const signatureVerified = rsaVerify(publicKeyObject, message,
    signature)
console.log('Signature valid:', signatureVerified)
```

In this sample, we start by importing the required modules (`crypto` and `fs`), and then we define the message that we want to sign.

Then, we load the private key from the file and compute the digital signature of the message with `rsaSign`. After that, we do the inverse, loading the public key and using that to verify the signature with `rsaVerify`.

The output, which is different whenever we use RSA-PSS for padding (because it's non-deterministic, unlike the RSA-PKCS#1 v1.5 padding, which returns the same output for each key and message pair), should look similar to the following, generated with a 4,096-bit key and not truncated:

```
Message: I owe Clare $100
Signature: OO9WKNZrsxBytvMIEqpYKXdy16iVv5USj614ZCvgymrU+Fb2SAKN
```

```
zWT81G0Qf4tJFvR2DJPM2GdUXaD6Ds8/IhsS+NB+mzyYUExGXR8oOx1cgTtvy27
Iezg4ck7GVuzzYhzxqD9dDUWPndi2drJK39IxOc+9hJf9sgVHy+hEya6yPLRofc
9n1UDUa/tBHwgEGzUzzGZBSFyjW9hYsCodm0bDNZe83byNhk9eXXcm/nC2ph4Km
lvZYa1d0Uq7nkQ/Zlzr8ix19PpGEGBgVkbu7esC3pvc7dazQ/mwqAIZ9frjx1
WHynA/++ROb7+9hsfqUdAEaG0n6OynTMVBIWWWhwawGC9zhj/OpxXnprwaVJdx
SocTZFcWcYa/5DFuNOjG9cwMTes6/0IjHEV1HBggRil+cTiD/Ro/G549G578v
WME+mW2SCK4zGvDA4DeutQAszJ6XWt2VfWdyLJ1i02dgpgDj5LpMJG2NYIaB2
HsmVLPne+ueUsFo42ireNxOhRrpwmg+JyfmQf9vRHQGNyh9Y/YYYsjOgkuYEZ
2wU4/oPJ9J6Woqh43eEtr3yQQxFWj23gcZ2LVC0K15OwrB6bk7UQ8zTe6XPfX
5vX2Tr3+qSL3LIsB5ugnbhT7m4Gt8zGQ4Z28goXxZNPBB0AkHmdNJsnyl3fSB
CP58ky7r4G5Cxo=
```
Signature valid: true

Note that the preceding code assumes that the private and public RSA keys are in files called `private.pem` and `public.pem`, respectively, and located in the same folder as our script. Your application will often need to load those in different ways, not from a file on disk.

> **Generating RSA Keys for Signing**
>
> The `private.pem` and `public.pem` files that we used in the preceding code sample are regular RSA keys that can be generated in the same way we generated them in *Chapter 5, Using Asymmetric and Hybrid Encryption in Node.js*, including with Node.js (using the code snippets included in that chapter) or with command-line tools such as OpenSSL. If you need to generate a new key pair quickly to run these code samples, you can do so with OpenSSL, as we saw in the previous chapter:
>
> ```
> $ openssl genrsa -out private.pem 4096
> $ openssl rsa -in private.pem -outform PEM -pubout
> -out public.pem
> ```
>
> Note that with RSA, although possible, you should avoid using the same key pair for both encryption and computing digital signatures, for security reasons.

Calculating the signature of large files with streams

As we saw in *Chapter 3, File and Password Hashing with Node.js* with hashing, the `rsaSign` and `rsaVerify` functions we've implemented here require that we load the entire message to sign or verify it in memory.

When you're dealing with large files, this may be a problem, as reading the entire document in memory can require a lot of resources. In those situations, it's often better to use the Node.js streaming APIs to read a file (or any other readable stream, such as data coming from an HTTP request's response) in chunks and pass that to the signing function.

With the `crypto` module in Node.js, we can create "signer" and "verifier" objects with `crypto.createSign` and `crypto.createVerify`, both of which implement the streaming interfaces and can be used by piping data into them.

You can find an example of how to compute the signature of a stream in Node.js in the `signatures-rsa-stream.js` file in this book's GitHub repository, in the `ch6-digital-signatures` folder; because it's fairly long, we won't replicate the entire code in this book. This file, which is thoroughly commented, looks very similar to the one we saw in *Chapter 3, File and Password Hashing with Node.js*, for calculating the SHA-256 digest of a stream, and follows the same patterns.

Using elliptic curves

As an alternative to RSA, we can leverage **ECC** to calculate the digital signature of a message too.

ECC has been growing in adoption and popularity over the last years, and the arguments in favor of using elliptic curves rather than RSA are very similar to the ones we presented in the context of data encryption in *Chapter 5, Using Asymmetric and Hybrid Encryption in Node.js*. In particular, ECC offers comparable levels of security to RSA with much smaller keys, which means that the resulting signatures are significantly smaller: this alone can be of strong relevance for many applications that need to use digital signatures. Additionally, using ECC can allow you to generate signatures faster than RSA.

In this chapter, we're going to look at two algorithms for digital signatures with elliptic curves, using the same curves we saw in the previous chapter:

- ECDSA using P-256 (prime256v1)
- EdDSA using Ed25519 (based on Curve25519)

ECDSA versus EdDSA

Elliptic Curve Digital Signature Algorithm (ECDSA) and **Edwards-curve Digital Signature Algorithm (EdDSA)** are two different signature algorithms, but both of them are based on ECC. Although there are significant differences in the algorithms behind them, as usual in this book, we won't get into the details of how they are implemented. However, it's important to point out that EdDSA, which is a newer algorithm, has some size and speed advantages over ECDSA, but it only works with certain kinds of curves, called "twisted Edwards curves," such as Curve25519 and Curve448. Other curves, including P-256, are used with ECDSA for digital signatures.

For a discussion on how to choose which curve to use, I recommend revisiting the relevant section on ECC in *Chapter 5, Using Asymmetric and Hybrid Encryption in Node.js.*

Using ECDSA and P-256 (prime256v1)

In this first example, we'll learn how to generate and verify a signature using ECDSA and the P-256 curve, which in Node.js is identified as prime256v1:

6.3: prime256v1Sign and prime256v1Verify (part of signatures-prime256v1.js)

```
const crypto = require('crypto')


function prime256v1Sign(privateKey, message) {
    return crypto.sign(
        'sha256', message, privateKey
    )
}


function prime256v1Verify(publicKey, message, signature) {
    return crypto.verify(
        'sha256', message, publicKey, signature
    )
}
```

The `prime256v1Sign` and `prime256v1Verify` functions have identical signatures to the `rsaSign` and `rsaVerify` ones we saw in the previous section. Their implementation looks very similar too, with the only difference that, in the `crypto.sign` and `crypto.verify` functions, for the `key` argument, we're passing the private and public keys (respectively) as-is, without defining any optional padding algorithm.

Because they have the same signature and options as `rsaSign` and `rsaVerify`, these two functions can also be used in the same way, with code that is identical to the one we saw in *Sample 6.2*, differing only in terms of the names of the functions being invoked (and, of course, in the fact that the keys that are used must be of type prime256v1!).

Generating P-256 Keys

Just like for RSA keys, you can generate P-256 ones (also called prime256v1) using the same code we saw in *Chapter 5, Using Asymmetric and Hybrid Encryption in Node.js*, with Node.js or with command-line tools such as OpenSSL.

For quickly generating P-256 keys with OpenSSL (1.1.0 or higher), you can use the following two commands:

```
$ openssl genpkey -algorithm ec -pkeyopt
ec_paramgen_curve:prime256v1 -out
private-prime256v1.pem
```

```
$ openssl pkey -in private-prime256v1.pem -pubout
-out public-prime256v1.pem
```

Note for macOS users: The built-in `openssl` command in macOS (at least up to Monterey, the latest version at the time of writing) does not include support for these commands. Instead, you will need to install a more recent build of OpenSSL from Homebrew.

If you run the entire code sample, which can be seen in this book's GitHub repository in the `signatures-prime256v1.js` file in the `ch6-digital-signatures` folder, you will see an output similar to this:

```
Message: I owe Clare $100
Signature: NTg2dxiE1g7gnLKqOT60j3WjkLkwyy5q7zb7vlLyajnYi5xeJfun
xVWhqdlAokZ71WpFp2/2uqOyu5RlKf7nBw==
Signature valid: true
```

The output has been reported in its entirety here so that you can see how the signature is significantly smaller than the one that's generated with RSA and a 4,096-bit key, as reported in full earlier in this chapter, yet both algorithms offer a similar degree of security. The smaller the size of the signature, which is due to the usage of smaller keys, can make ECDSA signatures easier to manage, especially in constrained environments.

Using EdDSA and Ed25519

For this final example, we're going to use EdDSA with Ed25519. As we mentioned in the previous chapter, both Ed25519 and X25519 (which we used to perform a key exchange) are based on Curve25519, although the keys are not compatible with each other.

> **Generating Ed25519 Keys**
>
> To generate Ed25519 (which are different from X25519 keys, like those used for ECDH key exchanges), you can once again use Node.js and the sample we saw in *Chapter 5, Using Asymmetric and Hybrid Encryption in Node.js*, or you can use a sufficiently recent version of OpenSSL (1.1.0 or higher) in the command line.
>
> To generate an Ed25519 key pair with OpenSSL, you can use the following commands:
>
> ```
> $ openssl genpkey -algorithm
> ed25519 -out private-ed25519.pem
> $ openssl pkey -in private-ed25519.pem -pubout
> -out public-ed25519.pem
> ```

The functions that generate and verify Ed25519 signatures using Node.js can be written as follows:

6.3: ed25519Sign and ed25519Verify (part of signatures-ed25519.js)

```
const crypto = require('crypto')


function ed25519Sign(privateKey, message) {
    return crypto.sign(
        null, message, privateKey
    )
}


function ed25519Verify(publicKey, message, signature) {
    return crypto.verify(
        null, message, publicKey, signature
    )
}
```

This example should be almost boring as the code is *almost* identical to the previous two! The only thing worth highlighting is that the first argument to `crypto.sign` and `crypto.verify`, the hashing algorithm, is `null`, and this is because using Ed25519, the hashing step is built into the digital signature algorithm and is not configurable by the end user.

When using `ed25519Sign` and `ed25519Verify`, make sure that you pass the private and public keys in `crypto.KeyObject` objects that contain a pair of keys of the `ed25519` type.

The full example, which includes using the preceding code (repeating *Sample 6.2* almost exactly) is available in this book's GitHub repository, in the `signatures-ed25519.js` file, in the `ch6-digital-signatures` folder.

With this code sample, we've completed our journey across all the major cryptographic operations we set ourselves to learn. The remainder of this chapter will cover the concept of how to tie a key pair to an identity, such as to a physical person or an organization, and why that is a significant problem.

Trust and certificates

In this and the previous chapters, we learned how public-key cryptography allows us to have secure communication with another person over an untrusted channel, and how, with digital signatures, we also get integrity, authentication, and non-repudiation. All those things are excellent; yet, before we end our dissertation around this topic, there's one last thing we need to cover.

The problem of trusting keys

Let's assume you need to send some confidential information to your friend Alex over the Internet, so you decide to build a solution that uses public-key cryptography. Before you can send Alex a message, you know you need to ask them for their public key. You decide that, for increased security, you want Alex to send you their public key in a message that is signed with their private key (that is, Alex's message contains their public key and a signature that can be verified with the very same public key). This will act as a guarantee that Alex is actually in possession of the corresponding private key.

We've talked about Man-in-the-Middle attacks before, and you know the risk: if the message Alex sends you isn't signed, someone else could intercept it and replace Alex's public key with another one (so, when you send a message to Alex later, the attacker can read it instead!). By requiring a signature on Alex's message – the one containing their public key – you know it couldn't have been tampered with. Everything should be fine now!

Except, there's a problem. When you get the message from Alex with their key, the only thing you know for sure is that it came from someone in possession of the private key that matches the public one the message itself contains, but you have no way to know that person was Alex. An attacker could have replaced both the message (the public key) and the signature, giving you a different public key and signing it with their private key.

When Alex sends you their public key and signs it with the corresponding private key, that is called "self-signing." It allows you to be sure that the other party does possess the private key they claim to have, but it does not give you any guarantee of the other party's identity. You may have heard of "self-signed certificates" before, such as when you're running your HTTPS server, and that's the very same concept.

The problem with authenticating the other party is a very serious one in real life too, such as in the context of TLS/HTTPS. When you visit a website, such as google.com, you type the domain name into your browser's address bar. The browser makes a request to a DNS server to get the IP of Google, such as 2.3.4.5, and then you connect to that IP. If the connection uses HTTPS, your browser performs a TLS key exchange and generates a shared key that is used to encrypt the traffic.

A problem could arise in case of an attack on the DNS infrastructure (this type of attack is called **DNS poisoning**). An attacker could make it so that when your browser resolves google.com, the DNS query returns a different IP, such as 9.8.7.6 – the address of a server that's owned by a bad actor. Your browser will then establish a TLS session, which will allow all the traffic to be encrypted with HTTPS, except that the other party isn't Google!

To solve this problem, we need to introduce a system that allows us to trust, and verify, who the other party claims to be. That is, we need to find a way to bind a public key with the identity of a real person or organization.

Public keys and certificates

So far, we've been talking about how public key cryptography requires two parties to exchange public keys so that they can send each other encrypted messages, perform key exchanges, and/or verify digital signatures. In reality, it's fairly uncommon for applications to deal with public keys alone (which are just random numbers or sequences of bytes) without any additional metadata or context.

In the case of TLS, and other protocols that leverage PKI (more on that soon), keys are normally embedded inside a **certificate**, which contains additional information on the key and other metadata. Other protocols and applications may use different formats to encapsulate keys and their metadata, but regardless of the format of the file that's used, the kind of additional information that is encoded is often similar.

Certificates are files that contain data encoded in the same PEM format we saw that's used for keys (ASN.1 encoded as DER). The following is an example (the middle of the certificate was truncated for brevity):

```
-----BEGIN CERTIFICATE-----
MIIE9jCCAt6gAwIBAgICECAwDQYJKoZIhvcNAQEL
```

```
[...]

agC53Q5HYOz8PMBBbL+9RrcKwjYr410UJI0=

-----END CERTIFICATE-----
```

Certificates can be fairly long and contain a lot of different data points. What is contained in each certificate varies, but the most common fields include a **subject** (what the certificate is for, such as what domain name), **validity bounds** (not before and not after/expiration), the **type of key** included (such as RSA or elliptic curve), what the key can be **used for** (for example, digital signatures, encrypting data, and/or wrapping keys), and a lot more.

For example, at the time of writing, when I connect to `microsoft.com` and decode the certificate, it begins with this:

Figure 6.1 – Part of the certificate for microsoft.com, decoded

There's a lot of information contained in the certificate and a lot more that is not shown in this screenshot. However, most of the interesting parts are there, including the RSA public key (see the value in `Subject Public Key Info`). Additionally, the `Subject` line says that the certificate is for the `www.microsoft.com` domain (see the value after `CN`; additional subjects/domains are defined in a different field).

Certificates alone don't solve the problem of trust. Anyone could generate an RSA key and then a certificate that says that such a key is to be trusted when connecting to `www.microsoft.com`; however, certificates allow us to embed additional data, including a **signature from a trusted party**.

Public Key Infrastructure

In cryptography, **Public Key Infrastructure (PKI)** is a complex set of technologies, processes, people, and policies that allow us to define the binding between a public key and an identity in the real world.

We could write an entire book about PKI – in fact, those have been written! We won't get into the details of PKI's inner workings, or even how to manage your own PKI (arguably, that's not something most developers will ever need to do); instead, we'll just provide a brief overview of how the system works.

To start, PKI is a centralized system, in which trust in every certificate is ultimately due to a **Certificate Authority (CA)**.

As we mentioned previously, certificates can include, among the various fields, a signature from a trusted party. In a PKI situation, that signature is calculated on the certificate's key and other fields, and it's generated by the CA directly, or by intermediate certificates that are signed by the CA.

For example, the certificate that `nytimes.com` shows at the time of writing is signed by the CA **Sectigo RSA Domain Validation Secure Server**, which itself is signed by **USERTrust RSA Certificate Authority**:

Path #1: Trusted

		nytimes.com
		Fingerprint SHA256: 5a718da6e2d2691e0e2dfded6cc0699af6e0a6489f195539bf21748857e3f7f7
1	Sent by server	Pin SHA256: WQ08Q1ELBHV75cuYqCSCkLxn9NtUbWG6/VKIhoStyLY=
		RSA 2048 bits (e 65537) / SHA256withRSA
		Sectigo RSA Domain Validation Secure Server CA
		Fingerprint SHA256: 7fa4ff68ec04a99d7528d5085f94907f4d1dd1c5381bacdc832ed5c960214676
2	Sent by server	Pin SHA256: 4a6cPehI7OG6cuDZka5NDZ7FR8a60d3auda+sKfg4Ng=
		RSA 2048 bits (e 65537) / SHA384withRSA
		USERTrust RSA Certification Authority Self-signed
		Fingerprint SHA256: e793c9b02fd8aa13e21c31228accb08119643b749c898964b1746d46c3d4cbd2
3	In trust store	Pin SHA256: x4QzPSC810K5/cMjb05Qm4k3Bw5zBn4lTdO/nEW/Td4=
		RSA 4096 bits (e 65537) / SHA384withRSA

Figure 6.2 – The certification path (one of the two) for the certificate for nytimes.com, as analyzed with Qualys SSL Labs (`https://ssllabs.com/`)

When your browser connects to `nytimes.com`, the chain of signatures is checked during the TLS handshake step and, if everything is verified correctly, you know that you're connecting to the server that hosts the New York Times' website. In this example, the "ultimate trust" comes from the "USERTrust" CA certificate.

However, if, with PKI, every certificate's trustworthiness comes from being signed by another certificate (a CA), we have a bit of a chicken-and-egg problem: who signs the "first" certificate, also called the **root certificate**? In reality, no one – or, to be precise, root CA certificates are **self-signed**, which means that their trust comes from within themselves. Those root certificates are included in the operating system or browser's **trust store**, which is a collection of certificates that are distributed with the base system (or with the web browser) and that are known to be trustworthy to the vendor.

On Windows, trusted root certificates are included in the Trusted Root Certificate Authorities Store, on macOS, they are included in the Keychain app, and on Linux, they are usually deployed to the `/usr/share/ca-certificates` folder (although this may change, depending on the distribution in use).

Those "official" trust stores contain only a handful of certificates. For example, the Mozilla CA list, which various Linux distributions, as well as apps such as Mozilla Firefox, rely on, at the time of writing includes just 143 certificates issued by 52 CAs (source: `https://wiki.mozilla.org/CA`), most of which are major corporations or governments.

This contributes to the highly centralized nature of PKI, especially the one that's used for the Web, and that is one of the main criticisms of this entire approach.

If you have ever hosted a website that is served securely over HTTPS/TLS, you know that you need to provide a certificate for encryption to work. As we saw previously, using self-signed certificates is always a (free) option, but because the browser can't find a trusted signature, these certificates display a warning every time users try to access your site, and the browser asks them to accept a security exception:

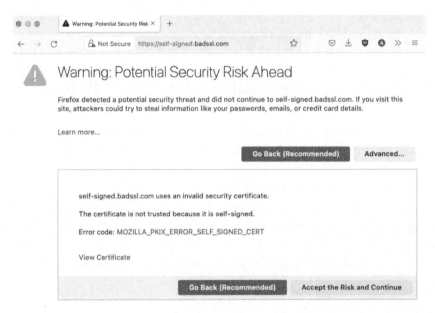

Figure 6.3 – An example of the warning message Mozilla Firefox shows when accessing a website that uses self-signed certificates

Although it's possible to obtain free certificates that are accepted by most clients thanks to projects such as Let's Encrypt (`https://letsencrypt.org/`), which is the product of a nonprofit organization created in 2012 and now sponsored by a consortium of tech companies, that was not always the case. Despite being required for all websites that wanted to use important security features such as HTTPS, certificates used to be very expensive, sometimes costing hundreds of dollars per year per domain name – and even now, if you need to acquire a certificate from a commercial organization (for example, because you can't use Let's Encrypt for a variety of reasons), you can expect to pay a lot of money.

Of course, everyone can create their own Certificate Authority with a self-signed root certificate, and then begin signing other certificates. However, unless your root certificate is included in the major trust stores (such as those managed by Microsoft, Apple, Mozilla, and Google), your root certificate and every certificate signed with that will appear as self-signed to your site's visitors, and it will trigger a warning, similar to the one shown in the previous example.

> **Creating Your Own Certificate Authority Using OpenSSL**
>
> This step-by-step guide by Jamie Nguyen explains how to create your own CA using OpenSSL, including creating a root certificate and optional intermediate ones that are used to sign individual client certificates: `https://bit.ly/crypto-yourca`. If you're interested in learning more about PKI, this is also an excellent opportunity to gain familiarity through hands-on exposure. Needless to say, this may be very helpful if you have a home lab too!
>
> Once you have generated a new CA, you can install the root certificate into your operating system's certificate trust store to begin trusting every certificate that's signed by your CA (and the intermediate CAs).
>
> Large organizations managing their PKIs have root CAs that they use to create certificates for internal sites and apps. Leveraging device management solutions (such as Microsoft Active Directory or InTune), the root CA certificate is then installed in every device that is managed by the organization, including laptops and phones. This allows the organization's IT team to generate certificates for any internal or external domain, without relying on (and paying) an external entity; by using device management solutions to distribute the CA certificate at scale, they ensure that every device that needs access to those resources can verify the certificates they issue.

New root CA certificates are continuously added to the root trust stores, but each situation is carefully evaluated, given the strong security implications of those decisions. Every CA is authorized to issue certificates for any subject (that is, any domain), so the organization that owns the CA needs to be trustworthy and have strong protections in place to secure the CA's private key. Having the ability to issue certificates can potentially allow an organization to set up fake websites to steal users' data or credentials, or even to transparently intercept and decrypt traffic to a website.

Because of the potential security risks, CAs that issue certificates for a domain must require that you provide proof of owning the domain you are requesting a certificate for. This can happen in multiple ways; for example, in the case of Let's Encrypt, the process is fully automated via the Certbot tool.

There have been multiple incidents that have caused organizations to stop trusting root CA certificates, including the following:

- In 2015, Google and other companies revoked the trust to CNNIC's certificate, China's main digital CA, removing it from their trust stores. This was in response to the CNNIC's root certificate being used to issue fake certificates for Google domains (source: `https://www.zdnet.com/article/google-banishes-chinas-main-digital-certificate-authority-cnnic/`).

Those certificates could have been used to intercept traffic from users visiting Google's web properties, transparently decrypting (and even modifying) the information by a Man-in-the-Middle such as an attacker or perhaps even the government. When fake certificates are signed by a trusted root CA, as they were in this case, the attacker could serve their certificate in place of Google's, and end users would see no warning of this: although the certificate being served by the web server would be different from Google's authentic one, users would not be able to notice the swap unless they actively dig into their browser's inner workings – something that can't be expected from anyone but some highly skilled users with particularly tight setups.

- In other cases, attackers successfully breached CAs and managed to obtain fake certificates from them. One notable example of this is the 2011 hack of DigiNotar, a Dutch CA that has since been shut down. In that instance, investigators found that attackers were able to issue more than 500 fake certificates. It's suspected that the Iranian government used those certificates to perform Man-in-the-Middle attacks and intercept the Internet traffic of its citizens, such as those accessing Gmail. To learn more, please go to `https://bit.ly/crypto-diginotar`.

Let's look at some of the alternative approaches.

Alternative approaches

The model we described previously, in which there's a centralized Certificate Authority at the center of the PKI and from which trust in all certificates is derived, is by far the most widely used – really, that's the only possibility for HTTPS today – but it's not entirely devoid of issues, real or potential.

The main points of criticism of this system stem from the fact it's a centralized solution, in which a small number of entities have outsized power over the entire PKI: those who own CA certificates that are included in default trust stores, along with those who control those trust stores. The world needs to trust that CAs do not begin to issue fake or fraudulent certificates and that the security measures they have in place are effective at defending against attackers, including highly sophisticated ones that may be state-sponsored – an increasingly common occurrence.

Additionally, from a more philosophical standpoint, the centralization that is in the CA-based approach is at odds with the decentralized nature of the Internet.

Web of Trust

Alternative, decentralized approaches have been proposed for decades. The most relevant example is the idea of the **Web of Trust**, which is implemented by GPG: in this model, there's no centralized authority that decides who to trust, but rather each person becomes involved in multiple "webs of trust."

In 1992, Phil Zimmermann explained the concept of the Web of Trust in the manual for the PGP software he created (PGP is the proprietary precursor to the open source GPG project):

> *As time goes on, you will accumulate keys from other people that you may want to designate as trusted introducers. Everyone else will each choose their own trusted introducers. And everyone will gradually accumulate and distribute with their key a collection of certifying signatures from other people, with the expectation that anyone receiving it will trust at least one or two of the signatures. This will cause the emergence of a decentralized fault-tolerant web of confidence for all public keys.*
>
> *– Philip Zimmermann, "PGP User's Guide Volume I: Essential Topics"*
> *(1992)*

For example, let's assume that you want to send a message to Alice. You would trust Alice's key if she gave it to you in person, but that didn't happen. However, you have received Bob's key in person, so you can trust his, and Bob received Alice's key and he trusts hers. In the Web of Trust model, you can then transitively trust Alice's key because Bob trusts it and you trust Bob's (note that transitive trust in the PGP/GPG model is limited to one degree, so you wouldn't automatically trust all the keys that Alice trusts). It's worth noting that in all these cases, "trusting a key" refers to creating and publishing a signature for the other person's key with your own.

People can meet in person at "key signing parties" to trust other persons' keys and expand their web of trust. Perhaps less common nowadays than they once were, you may still find them in areas with a large enough number of tech-minded people.

In reality, the Web of Trust approach never took off outside of PGP/GPG, and even in that space, it's not relied on by everyone. There are multiple reasons for that, but they can be summed up by saying that such a system is inefficient (every person needs to build their own web of trust, which is time-consuming and complex), doesn't scale (the keys you trust are limited to those of the people you've met in person or their in-person connections), and it's slow (especially when it requires in-person meetups). Add to that the fact that the Web of Trust is complicated, both in terms of theory and in the practical sense, including the process of signing keys and verifying the other person's identity correctly beforehand.

Newer approaches

At its core, GPG needed to solve two problems: discovering another person's key and trusting that it corresponds to the real individual. For the former, you can use one of the public GPG key servers, such as `https://keyserver.ubuntu.com/`, where you can look up any person or their email address and get the matching GPG keys. Because anyone can generate a GPG key for any email address, the Web of Trust model allows someone's keys to be verified by others'. GPG came out in 1999 and its predecessor, PGP, was published in 1991, so those systems were possibly the best options available at the time.

Today, social media offers another approach to distributing public keys (including public GPG keys) and having them trusted at the same time. As an example, you can often see something similar to the following screenshots on the Twitter bio or personal website of journalists, who rely on GPG (or other secure apps such as Signal) to safely communicate with tipsters:

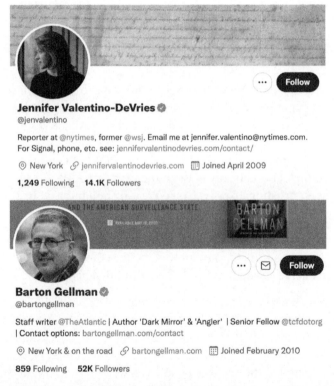

Figure 6.4 – Twitter profiles of journalists @jenvalentino (The New York Times) and @bartongellman (The Atlantic). Their bios contain links to pages on their websites where you can find ways to contact them securely, such as Signal phone numbers and GPG keys

In this case, you can trust that the key is correct because it's highlighted in the social media profile of the person who's publishing it. The reporters in the preceding screenshot have even verified their profiles on Twitter (notice the blue checkmarks next to their names), further pointing out that their true identity is confirmed. Even for those who do not have a verified profile on a social media platform, having an established, years-long presence on the platform and multiple references to that can be used by others to establish trust.

Building on the idea that established social media profiles can be used to build a trusted digital identity, and so distribute trusted public keys, the website **Keybase** contains people's keys and offers a built-in, encrypted messaging platform.

For example, my profile on Keybase is `https://keybase.io/italypaleale`:

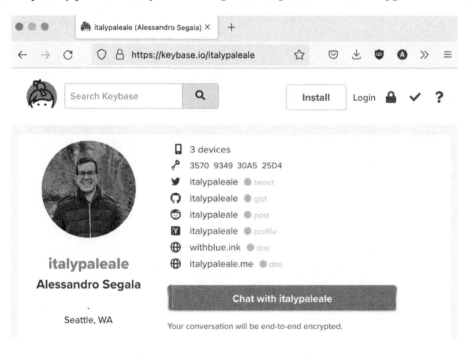

Figure 6.5 – My Keybase profile, showing the fingerprint of my GPG key and verified links to other social media profiles and domain names

Here, you can see my GPG key (fingerprint: `0x3570934930A525D4`) and proofs that link my Keybase account with my other social media profiles. *It's worth pointing out that including your GPG key in a book that's been published under your name like I just did is yet another way to add trust to that – although you may find simpler ways to do so!*

Summary

In this chapter, we analyzed the last major class of cryptographic operations that we will be covering in this book – digital signatures. We've seen how they guarantee the integrity of a message, authenticate a sender, and prevent repudiation. We then saw examples of creating and validating RSA, ECDSA, and EdDSA digital signatures with Node.js.

In the second part of this chapter, we covered the problem of binding a public key to the identity of a real person or organization, and why it is significant. We looked at possible ways to address that problem, including PKI and the Web of Trust, and we learned about certificates.

Throughout this book so far, we've focused on using JavaScript in a Node.js context. The next and last section of this book will cover how to use the main cryptographic operations we've learned about inside a web browser, using JavaScript and various WebCrypto APIs.

Part 3 – Cryptography in the Browser

In this last section, we will revise the concepts introduced in the previous two, this time showing examples that use frontend JavaScript code designed to run within a web browser.

This section comprises the following chapters:

7

Introduction to Cryptography in the Browser

We couldn't end a book about cryptography in JavaScript writing just about Node.js and not covering the other side of the coin: web browsers.

The ability to build browser-based applications in JavaScript that use cryptography is a relatively recent addition to the Web Platform, but one that is very much welcome as it allows you to create new kinds of applications, including those leveraging **end-to-end encryption** (**E2EE**). Yet, it also comes with some additional challenges, some of which are common to all client-side applications, and some that are unique because we're running our code in a web browser and distributing it over the Internet.

In this chapter, we're going to cover the following main topics:

- An overview of cryptography in the browser: the advantages, the challenges and risks, and how it's gotten much easier for developers to use thanks to the various Web Crypto APIs and WebAssembly.

- Managing binary data in the browser, including how to use `ArrayBuffer` objects and typed arrays, and how to encode and decode to/from base64 and hex.

- Lastly, we'll look at how cryptographic keys are stored in `CryptoKey` objects, and how they can be generated, imported, or exported.

Technical requirements

All the code samples for this chapter can be found in this book's GitHub repository at `https://bit.ly/crypto-ch7`.

Playground

To make it easier to build and test the code samples in these last two chapters, which often include third-party modules from npm, we have set up a "playground" that runs within your browser. You can access it at `https://bit.ly/crypto-playground`.

In Node.js

While this chapter and the next will be referring to JavaScript code written for web browsers, the same APIs have been made available in Node.js as a compatibility layer since version 15, released in October 2020.

In Node.js, the Web Crypto APIs are available in the `webcrypto` object in the `crypto` module.

For example, take this snippet of JavaScript code for the browser, which we'll be covering later in this chapter:

```
window.crypto.getRandomValues(array)
```

To use it in Node.js (15+), change from `window.crypto` to the `webcrypto` object, which can be imported from the `crypto` module:

```
const crypto = require('crypto').webcrypto
crypto.getRandomValues(array)
```

The Node.js implementation of Web Crypto should be fully compatible with the one in the Web Platform; plus, it comes with some additional capabilities. For more information on using Web Crypto in Node.js, you can look at the official documentation: `https://nodejs.org/api/webcrypto.html`.

About cryptography in the browser – uses and challenges

Throughout all the previous chapters of this book, we've learned about using common cryptographic operations in JavaScript in the context of a Node.js application – so, for code that (for the most part) runs on a server.

However, an increasing number of JavaScript applications that use cryptography are now running on the client side, inside a web browser. Not only are these growing in number, but also in terms of their capabilities and relevance.

The main advantage of performing cryptography inside clients is that it enables scenarios that are not possible otherwise for web applications, including the use of E2EE. This allows data to never leave the client in an unencrypted state and makes it impossible for a web server, and conversely for a service provider, to read the contents of encrypted messages – although note that metadata may still be exposed (for a refresher, see the description of the various layers of cryptography in *Chapter 1, Cryptography for Developers*). E2EE is considered the gold standard of protecting sensitive information, even when it's stored on remote servers, offering – when implemented correctly – the best security and privacy.

E2EE is not a novel concept, but until recently, it was primarily the domain of native applications. With advancements in the Web Platform, it's now possible to write apps that run entirely within a web browser and that are perfectly capable of performing all (or almost all) cryptographic operations, with great performance too.

The most relevant examples of applications that leverage in-browser cryptography include those offering E2EE cloud storage services. One of the first to gain significant adoption (but possibly for the wrong reasons, such as piracy) was MEGA, which launched in 2013. Other products and services in this category include Sync.com, SpiderOak, and Nextcloud.

Another area where we see significant (and growing) usage of in-browser E2EE is communication tools. Some examples include the ProtonMail encrypted email service, the WhatsApp web client, and the communication features of apps such as Keybase (which we encountered in the previous chapter as a tool used to exchange public keys).

Lastly, worth mentioning here are all the **dApps**, or "decentralized apps," which are those based on decentralized technologies such as blockchains. At the time of writing, this is a very nascent field, with lots of growth opportunities, but also many challenges. Earlier in this book, we briefly mentioned how blockchains rely heavily on cryptography, especially hashing and digital signatures: the latter are used extensively when committing transactions/messages. All dApps, then, make extensive use of cryptography in the browser, especially the asymmetric kind.

Challenges of cryptography in the browser

As we've seen throughout the previous chapters of this book, implementing solutions based on cryptography always comes with several challenges for developers. Even when you're not writing your own implementation of a cryptographic algorithm (*something we made you promise in this book's introduction to never, ever do!*), you need to pick the right class of operations, then choose among various algorithms, and oftentimes pick the correct options for using them too.

When implementing cryptography inside a client-side app, there are some **additional challenges** that developers need to take into account, which are further amplified because their code is meant to run in a web browser.

Do not include shared secrets

To start, you cannot include secrets in client-side apps. For example, you cannot include symmetric keys that are used to authenticate messages from the server (such as with HMAC); you will need to rely heavily on public-key cryptography instead.

Keep in mind that this first challenge applies to all apps running on a client, whether it's JavaScript executed by a web browser or native apps written in C/C++: even if the app is distributed as a compiled binary (rather than source code such as JavaScript), it can still be de-compiled or otherwise inspected, so you shouldn't rely on compilation alone to protect your secrets.

An alternative approach, which is somewhat better but still not completely safe, is to make your application fetch a shared secret from the server at runtime (rather than hardcoding it in your JavaScript code) and keep that in memory.

This is especially an option if you need to distribute secrets that are specific to each user: for example, a symmetric encryption key that is only used to encrypt data belonging to the logged-in user. This way, if a user finds a way to extract the secret, they still won't be able to access other users' information. You should still assume that users will be able to find their key if they wanted to: reading data stored in memory is always possible with apps that allow inspectingthe state of any other process running on your machine; in the case of web apps, this can be a simple browser extension too.

There's no persistent local storage

A challenge that is more specific to apps that run the browser is that you cannot rely on persistent local storage, unlike native desktop or mobile apps which can always store files on disk.

While your app can certainly store data in the browser's `localStorage` or similar places (in the past, cookies were often misused for this purpose), those aren't guaranteed to be persistent: it's very easy for a user to clear all data from the local storage or cookies, for example. More importantly, things stored in those ways are tied to a web browser and don't roam across browsers and devices, so what's stored inside the Edge browser in your laptop isn't synced with Safari on your iPhone.

This can be an issue in multiple cases, such as if you want to maintain a key stored locally on the user's machine.

You can't rely on the key to always be available on the user's browser, so instead, you should wrap that key with a symmetric cipher (likely using a key encryption key, or wrapping key, that is derived from a passphrase typed by the user) and then store the wrapped (encrypted) key on your servers. When the user needs the key, they will retrieve the wrapped key by requesting it from the server, and then unwrap it locally in the browser (this generally requires the user to type a passphrase again, since those can't be stored locally either).

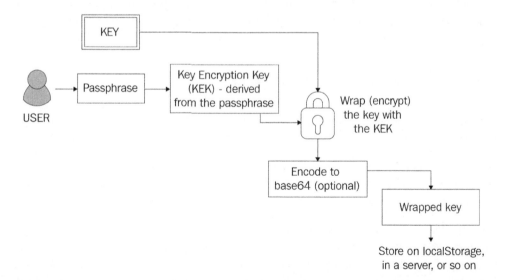

Figure 7.1 – Flow for wrapping (encrypting) a key with a Key Encryption Key (KEK) that is derived from a user-supplied passphrase. The wrapped key can be safely stored on localStorage or in a remote server

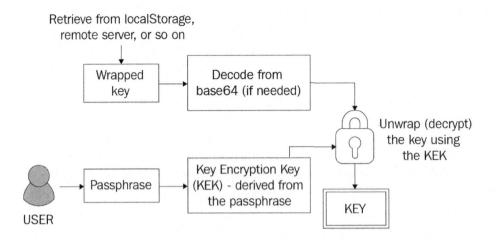

Figure 7.2 – Flow for unwrapping (decrypting) a key stored in localStorage or a remote server using
a Key Encryption Key (KEK) that is derived from a user-supplied passphrase

Note that at the time of writing, several APIs are being developed by browser vendors
to finally allow full, non-sandboxed filesystem access, including the File System Access
API (see `https://web.dev/file-system-access/`). Once standardized and
implemented by all major browsers, and after sufficient time for enough users to update
their browsers and OSes, these APIs may finally offer a solution to this problem, allowing
persistent storage that isn't tied to a specific browser (but that still doesn't automatically
roam to other devices, such as users' phones).

Cross-site scripting and other attacks

Another challenge that is specific to a browser environment is around security and, in
particular, the fact that there are too many ways for a malicious actor to inject their code
into your application.

The simplest example is with **Cross-Site Scripting** (**XSS**) attacks, which are very common
in the real world. With an XSS attack, an attacker can inject additional JavaScript code
that is executed by users of your app.

These attacks, such as XSS and others, aren't specific to apps that use in-browser
cryptography, yet they can have especially catastrophic consequences for them, for
example, allowing the theft of other users' private keys. While you should always do your
best to prevent XSS attacks, you need to be especially careful when your browser-based
app deals with high-value targets such as encryption keys.

> **Cross-Site Scripting (XSS) Attacks**
>
> To learn more about XSS attacks, and how to protect your app against them, a good starting point is this page on the OWASP's website: `https://bit.ly/crypto-xss`.

Ensuring the integrity of the code that's delivered to the client

One last challenge with using browser-based cryptography has to do with the Web's infrastructure, and while it can be mitigated, it hasn't been fully fixed yet.

The nature of all browser-based apps is that their code is downloaded from a server every time you use them, transparently to the user, and it's executed right away. The problem arises when an attacker finds a way to modify the JavaScript code that you're downloading: for example, they could inject some additional code that allows them to steal your private keys from your browser. This can happen in two ways.

First, they could hack the server where the code is stored and modify your JavaScript files at rest there. We'll assume that you have enough security measures in place to prevent this from happening.

The second, more insidious way, is to perform a **Man-in-the-Middle (MitM)** attack, such as those we've seen in *Chapter 6, Digital Signatures with Node.js and Trust*, in which someone intercepts the traffic from the server to your web browser and changes the JavaScript code that you're downloading.

The good news is that there are enough mitigations in place to make attacks such as these very hard to perform successfully. If your code is downloaded from a web server that uses HTTPS (and, as we'll see later, using the Web Crypto APIs makes that a requirement), then the connection is secured with TLS, and certificates and PKI are used to ensure the identity of the remote server and keep you safe in case of DNS poisoning attacks (as we saw in the second part of the previous chapter).

The bad news is that, just as we saw in the previous chapter, these attacks have been within reach of sophisticated actors such as government-sponsored ones.

The fast-evolving nature of the Web, where code changes continuously, and its decentralized nature, made of multiple ISPs causing different clients to go through different hops to connect to a server, makes detecting MitM attacks such as these particularly challenging. This is especially true for targeted attacks, such as those against single organizations or individuals (for example, a specific business or a political dissident).

In addition to the mitigations that are part of the web's infrastructure, including the usage of HTTPS/TLS, your application can rely on additional ones such as **Subresource Integrity** (**SRI**). All modern web browsers support an additional `integrity` attribute on the HTML `script` and `link` tags that allows you to include the checksum of the script or stylesheet that is being downloaded. When the SRI `integrity` attribute is present, before executing the script or applying the stylesheet, the browser must compute the checksum, and if it mismatches, it must reject the asset. The following is an example:

```
<script src="https://example.com/myscript.js"
    integrity="sha256-L3pIZiyaLC7K+ZqV0a0mSG5PdJewKLA5CTwc7FDo
iYQ"
></script>
```

This HTML tag tells the browser to load a script from `https://example.com/myscript.js`, which should have the SHA-256 hash highlighted in the preceding code (base64-encoded). If the browser receives a script with a different checksum, it will reject it.

To save you from managing SRI tags manually in your HTML files, your bundler may offer that capability built-in or through plugins. For example, with Webpack, you can use the `webpack-subresource-integrity` plugin.

Using SRI is particularly helpful to ensure that scripts that are loaded from external resources (such as CDNs) are exactly what you expect them to be, and it's effective at detecting whether someone is modifying the file maliciously (that is, a hacked remote server) and even if there's an MitM attack.

The limitation of SRI is that the expected checksum is hardcoded in the HTML file, so it's less helpful if the scripts/stylesheets are served from the same server as the HTML file. If an attacker managed to break into your server or perform an MitM on your domain to change the content of a JavaScript file, chances are they can very likely modify the checksum in the HTML file too.

Some developers have even begun using alternative, sometimes creative, approaches to publish the checksums of the files that are part of their browser-based apps, such as sharing them on Twitter (in this case, Twitter is used as a neutral third party and it's assumed that tweets can't be altered). The problem with activities like these is that, despite being very effective, they are not built into web browsers and require users to manually verify the checksums if they have any concerns, limiting their scale.

In all openness, the risks that have been exposed in these last few paragraphs (connected to the fact that there's no way to safely sign a browser-based app like you can sign a native executable) make the biggest argument against performing cryptography in the browser. Despite all the mitigations, with the current state of the Web Platform, they cannot be removed altogether. Whether this is a deal-breaker for you depends on your threat model: what you're protecting and who your adversaries are. For the developers of the Signal messaging app, for example, these risks were enough for deciding not to publish a web-based app, as they explained in a reply to a user on their forums: `https://bit.ly/crypto-signal-web`.

Building browser-based apps that use cryptography

Developers have been using JavaScript to build entire apps that run within a web browser for almost two decades, using what we now call the **Jamstack** (which stands for JavaScript, reusable APIs, and Markup). Google's Gmail was launched in 2004, and while it was not the very first example of such an app (the technology that made it possible, the XMLHTTPRequest APIs, were introduced as early as 1999), it was arguably the first one to reach the masses.

Yet, in-browser cryptography lagged behind, with mature apps appearing only a decade later, needing significant improvements on the Web Platform first.

As we've briefly mentioned throughout this book, cryptographic algorithms depend a lot on calculations with very large numbers, and that's especially true for public-key ones such as RSA or ECC. It turns out that dealing with very large numbers is something JavaScript, as a programming language, is terrible at – you may recall that JavaScript only supports one kind of numbers, and they are all floating-point ones, which can't be used to store large numbers with precision. In fact, in JavaScript, you will lose precision when storing a number bigger than $2^{53}-1$ (the value of the `Number.MAX_SAFE_INTEGER` constant).

Until the introduction of the native Web Crypto APIs in 2014, developers looking at implementing cryptography on the client side had to rely on pure JavaScript libraries such as JSBN, BN.js, or SJCL. Despite being heavily optimized, all those libraries were limited by having to work without native support for large integers. Combined with JavaScript runtimes that, on their own, were not as optimized as they are today, you may begin to see why performing complex cryptographic operations in the browser a decade ago was difficult and slow, if not outright impossible. As a personal story, in 2014, while working at a start-up, my team and I tried to implement a solution based on one of those cryptographic libraries for SRP (an authentication protocol that doesn't involve sending passwords to a server), and our proof-of-concept caused Google Chrome to freeze and then crashed the entire browser!

Thankfully, times have changed – the Web Platform has evolved significantly and we are now at the point where cryptography in the browser is essentially as capable as it is in native applications.

The Web Crypto APIs and WebAssembly

The modern way to perform cryptography in the browser is to rely on the **Web Crypto APIs**, which include built-in support for many of the algorithms we've seen in this book. All modern desktop and mobile browsers (that is, not counting the now-deprecated Internet Explorer, which does have some partial support too) have been shipping with them for many years, offering a guarantee of broad support. Because these APIs rely on native implementations, they are also very fast and secure.

One important thing to note is that the Web Crypto APIs only work within **secure contexts**. This means that they can only be used by websites that are served on a secure connection (using HTTPS/TLS) or on localhost; this decision was made for security reasons, as an additional mitigation to some of the challenges described earlier in this chapter.

> **Browser Support for Web Crypto**
>
> At the time of writing, general support for the Web Crypto APIs is available on all modern desktop and mobile browsers, but some minor implementation differences may exist. You should always consult the browser support tables on websites such as MDN and Can I Use to make sure that your code runs on all of your target browsers:
> ```
> https://developer.mozilla.org/docs/Web/API/
> SubtleCrypto
> ```
> ```
> https://caniuse.com/?search=SubtleCrypto.
> ```

For those algorithms that aren't natively supported, the modern Web Platform offers the option of using **WebAssembly** too. In the next chapter, we are going to use implementations that leverage WebAssembly when needed, such as for Argon2 hashing.

> **About WebAssembly**
>
> WebAssembly (also called **wasm** from the file extension) is a portable and efficient binary format that runs code "natively" within a web browser. With WebAssembly, it's possible to compile native libraries (usually written in C/C++ or Rust, but there is some level of support for other programming languages too) and run them within a web browser, oftentimes faster than JavaScript code. This can be especially useful when you're leveraging cryptography: with WebAssembly, it's possible to bring the reference implementations of algorithms that are not natively available in the Web Crypto APIs, and they are executed at speeds that are close to native, with full support for things such as native big integers.
>
> To learn more about WebAssembly, you can look at MDN: `https://developer.mozilla.org/docs/WebAssembly`.
>
> Note, however, that while applications that use WebAssembly are compiled, they still run within the context of a web browser, so all the security considerations that we looked at in the previous section still apply, including the fact that it's not appropriate to include secrets in .wasm files and that they are not signed.

Lastly, you can also look for pure JavaScript implementations for almost any algorithm, with a very high chance of finding a module on npm for each. While pure JavaScript code is almost always slower than WebAssembly (and much slower than the Web Crypto APIs), thanks to advancements in the Web Platform and the browsers' JavaScript runtimes, those libraries should provide acceptable performance nowadays.

With this, we're now ready to start looking at some code and cover the topics we mentioned in *Chapter 2, Dealing with Binary and Random Data*, this time in the context of the web browser. In the next section, we'll look at how to handle binary data in JavaScript in the browser, including encoding and decoding UTF-8 strings and using base64 and hex encodings. We'll also look at how to generate random data.

Binary data in the browser

In *Chapter 2, Dealing with Binary and Random Data*, we saw how, in Node.js, binary data is typically stored in `Buffer` objects and how those contain utilities to encode to, and decode from, strings too. Sadly, the `Buffer` API is one that, to this day, remains specific to Node.js, while the Web Platform opted for a different (more flexible, but possibly more complex) approach.

Buffers and typed arrays in the browser

In the JavaScript specifications supported by web browsers, binary data is stored inside buffers (*which is not the same as* Buffer *objects in Node.js!*) and is accessed through views such as typed arrays.

The ArrayBuffer object implements buffers as a chunk of fixed-length data. You can't access data inside an ArrayBuffer object directly, and there are only a few methods and properties in this object that you need to know about:

- You can create a new ArrayBuffer object with the new ArrayBuffer(length) constructor, where length is the size in bytes of the buffer to allocate (which can't be changed later). The new buffer is initialized so that all the bytes are zeroed. For example, this creates a new ArrayBuffer object with 16 bytes, all of which are 0s:

```
const ab = new ArrayBuffer(16)
```

- byteLength is a (read-only) property that returns the length of the buffer in bytes. With the object we created previously, ab.byteLength would return 16.

- slice(start, [end]) is a method that returns a new ArrayBuffer object whose contents are copied from the byte start up to end (or the rest of the buffer if no end is specified). Note that this method creates a copy of the data of the underlying buffer: if you modify the copied object, the original buffer remains unchanged.

This is essentially all that you need to know about ArrayBuffer objects, which are really of limited use by themselves.

To be able to access and modify the data inside the buffer, we need to use a **view**, which provides the context, such as the data type. The most common views are typed arrays, which allow us to access the buffer's underlying data as the usual numeric types of strongly typed languages such as C, Java, and so on. You can also create custom views with the DataView object.

The built-in typed arrays have descriptive names that indicate how data from the buffer is interpreted, for example, Int8Array, Uint16Array, Float32Array, BigInt64Array, and so on. While they can all be useful in their applications, in our case, where we just need to safely manage binary data as byte arrays, we're interested in only one: Uint8Array.

With the Uint8Array view, we can access each byte in the buffer individually, byte by byte, as numbers between 0 and 255; this is equivalent to an array of uint8_t in C/C++.

You can create a `Uint8Array` object in multiple ways, including these four which are of particular relevance to us:

- From an `ArrayBuffer`:

```
const view = new Uint8Array( new ArrayBuffer(16) )
```

- From a length, which creates a new, zeroed buffer internally:

```
const view = new Uint8Array(16)
```

- From another typed array (even of different types):

```
const view = new Uint8Array( new Int32Array(16) )
```

- From an array of numbers, each between 0 and 255:

```
const view = new Uint8Array([1, 2, 3])
```

Most importantly, once you have a view such as `Uint8Array` on your buffer, you can access and manipulate data by addressing each byte using the standard array syntax; for example:

```
const view = new Uint8Array(16)
view[0] = 1
console.log(view[15]) // Result: 0
```

The preceding example sets the first byte (at position 0) to a value of 1 and then reads the last byte (at position 15), which is 0 because, by default, all buffers are initialized with all bytes set to zero.

Typed arrays are just like any other array, so you can also iterate through all the values with a `for` loop to view or modify the buffer's data:

```
for (let i = 0; i < 16; i++) {
    // Do something with view[i]
}
```

Each typed array contains the same properties and methods we found on the `ArrayBuffer` objects: `byteLength` and `slice(start, [end])`.

Additionally, there are quite a few more properties and methods, which you can always find in the documentation at https://developer.mozilla.org/docs/Web/ JavaScript/Reference/Global_Objects/Uint8Array. The following are the most relevant to us:

- The buffer property (read-only) returns an ArrayBuffer object pointing to the underlying buffer. It's an easy way to "revert" from a Uint8Array view to an ArrayBuffer. The following example will print true because it's the same object:

```
const ab = new ArrayBuffer(16)
const view = new Uint8Array(ab)
console.log(view.buffer === ab) // Result: true
```

- The length property (read-only) returns the number of elements in the array; with 8-bit views such as Uint8Array, this is always equivalent to byteLength.

The last useful thing to know is how to concatenate multiple Uint8Array objects. As we mentioned previously, the size of each ArrayBuffer (and thus Uint8Array) is fixed and cannot be extended. However, you can create new typed arrays that are concatenated from others by using the array spread operator:

```
const view1 = new Uint8Array([1, 2, 3])
const view2 = new Uint8Array([4, 5, 6])
const merged = new Uint8Array([...view1, ...view2])
```

The result is a merged array that contains 6 bytes: [1, 2, 3, 4, 5, 6].

Typed Arrays and Node.js

Although uncommonly used, all these objects and APIs for managing binary data are also available on Node.js, including typed arrays (such as Uint8Array) and ArrayBuffer objects. These can be used in those instances when you want compatibility with JavaScript code that was written for the web browser.

In Node.js, not only is it possible to convert a Buffer object into a typed array and vice versa, but Buffer objects in Node.js are also Uint8Array and ArrayBuffer instances. You can read more about how to convert between the various objects, the implementation details, and the API differences in the official documentation: https://nodejs.org/api/ buffer.html#buffer_buffers_and_typedarrays.

Encoding to base64 and hex

Unlike in Node.js, where `Buffer` objects have built-in routines for converting to and from base64 and hex, there isn't a similar built-in JavaScript method that is available in web browsers.

To be precise, there are two legacy methods to convert to and from base64: `atob` ("ASCII-to-base64") and `btoa` ("base64-to-ASCII"). However, these functions are optimized for ASCII strings and do not work well with binary data or even just Unicode strings. The MDN documentation for the `btoa` method explains this issue in more detail: `https://developer.mozilla.org/docs/Web/API/btoa`. The bottom line, however, is that the two built-in methods, `atob` and `btoa`, do not always work correctly, do not support buffers or typed arrays, and are considered deprecated.

To convert from `Uint8Array` to and from **base64**, you can use the following methods:

- Functions such as those available in the MDN documentation: `https://developer.mozilla.org/docs/Glossary/Base64` (especially relevant is the example that uses typed arrays).

- One of the many packages published on npm, which vary in features such as support for different base64 charsets (such as base64 "standard" and base64 URL-safe). Some examples from npm include `@aws-sdk/util-base64-browser`, `arraybuffer-fns`, and `arraybuffer-encoding`, which we'll be using in the code samples for this book.

Likewise, for converting `Uint8Array` to and from **hex**, you can use a variety of packages from npm, including `arraybuffer-fns` and `arraybuffer-encoding`, which we mentioned previously for base64 encoding.

Generating random data

Continuing with updating the knowledge we acquired in *Chapter 2, Dealing with Binary and Random Data*, this time in the context of a web browser, the next step is to generate sequences of random bytes.

Thankfully for us, this requires just two lines of code using the Web Crypto APIs:

```
const array = new Uint8Array(10)
window.crypto.getRandomValues(array)
```

The `crypto.getRandomValues()` method accepts a typed array (such as a `Uint8Array`) with a buffer of a given size (10 bytes in this example) and fills it with random data. After running the preceding snippet, if you print the contents of `array`, you will see that it contains a sequence of 10 random numbers, each between 0 and 255.

> **Global Crypto Object**
>
> Note that in this case, as in all the other code samples in this chapter and the next, it's not strictly necessary to refer to the global `crypto` object with the `window.crypto` notation – just using `crypto` would be enough. However, we'll continue to use `window.crypto` as a best practice.

One thing you may notice is that, unlike the equivalent method in Node.js, the one that's implemented in the browser is **synchronous**. This is made possible by leveraging a pseudo-random number generator (PRNG) inside the browser that reduces the need to fetch entropy from the operating system (which could be a blocking operation). The key takeaway here is that `getRandomValues` is optimized for speed and for being non-blocking, rather than for providing high amounts of entropy.

The consequence is that the `getRandomValues` method in Web Crypto should not be used to generate things that require high entropy (that is, good randomness), such as encryption keys. The MDN documentation states the following regarding this:

> *Don't use* `getRandomValues()` *to generate encryption keys. Instead, use the* `generateKey()` *method.*

(Source: `https://developer.mozilla.org/en-US/docs/Web/API/Crypto/getRandomValues#usage_notes`)

This is a perfect lead-in for our next section, in which we'll look at the APIs inside Web Crypto that can be used to generate, derive, import, and export keys, including the `generateKey` method mentioned previously.

Keys in Web Crypto

Using the Web Crypto APIs, cryptographic keys are stored inside `CryptoKey` objects, which are used for both symmetric and asymmetric (private or public) keys. There are additional methods that allow us to generate, derive, import, and export keys that are stored in `CryptoKey` objects.

The CryptoKey object

All cryptographic keys that are used with Web Crypto APIs are contained in `CryptoKey` objects, which also determine what operations are possible with the keys and whether they're extractable.

In particular, a `CryptoKey` object contains the following properties, which are all read-only:

- `type` is a string that indicates the type of the key. Its possible values are `'public'` and `'private'` for each part of an asymmetric key, and `'secret'` for symmetric keys.

- `algorithm` is an object that contains information about the algorithm the key can be used for, as well as extra parameters. We'll learn more about these options later in this section.

- `extractable` is a Boolean that is true if the key can be extracted/exported. For keys that are living in memory for a long time and don't need to be exported, it's useful to set this flag to `false`, which helps protect the key in case of a compromise (for example, due to XSS attacks).

- `usages` is an array of strings that controls what operations can be performed with the key. This is also something that can be used to protect keys in case of compromises (or even just in the case of bugs!).

  For example, if a `CryptoKey` object that contains a key of the `'private'` type has `'sign'` as a flag in the `usages` parameter, but not `'decrypt'`, then the key can only be used for creating signatures but not decrypting messages. Rather than listing all the possible options here, for every method we'll analyze in this chapter and the next we'll mention what flags they require for keys.

Generating keys

To generate a new symmetric key or asymmetric key pair, you can use the `crypto.subtle.generateKey()` method.

`crypto.subtle`

In Web Crypto, all lower-level cryptographic primitives (including all the functions to encrypt, decrypt, sign, verify, and so on) are contained in the `subtle` property of the `window.crypto` object, which is an instance of the `SubtleCrypto` class.

The "subtle" adjective in the name was chosen to remind developers that these are low-level APIs and have the potential to be misused, with lots of subtle risks. But don't fear! With the help of this book and what you've learned so far, you should be able to use these "subtle" APIs with enough confidence (yet always with a healthy dose of caution).

The signature of the `generateKey` method is as follows:

```
const keyPromise = window.crypto.subtle.generateKey(algorithm,
extractable, usages)
```

The last two parameters, `extractable` and `usages`, are the ones we explained in the previous pages: `extractable` is a Boolean that controls whether the key can be exported, while `usages` is an array of strings indicating what the key can be used for.

The `algorithm` parameter, on the other hand, is an object that contains the algorithm and details of the key to generate:

- To generate a symmetric key for **AES**, pass an object containing two properties: {`name, length`}.

   The `name` property is a string with the AES variant to use, including the mode of operation. The supported values are `'AES-CBC'`, `'AES-GCM'`, `'AES-CTR'`, or `'AES-KW'`. We've analyzed the first two (CBC and GCM) at length in *Chapter 4, Symmetric Encryption in Node.js*, where we also mentioned CTR (a streaming cipher similar to GCM but not authenticated). The last option, AES-KW, is the algorithm for key wrapping based on RFC 3394 that we described in that chapter too.

   The `length` property controls the size of the key to generate, in bits. This is `128`, `192`, or `256`.

- You can also generate an **RSA** key pair by passing an object containing four properties: {`name, modulusLength, publicExponent, hash`}.

   First, `name` is a string that indicates the algorithm the key will be used for. For RSA keys that are used for encrypting, specify `'RSA-OAEP'` – this is the only option for encryption as the Web Crypto specifications don't support the legacy PKCS#1 v1.5 padding (for a refresher on these options, take a look at *Chapter 5, Using Asymmetric and Hybrid Encryption in Node.js*). If the RSA key is for use with digital signatures, you can specify either `'RSASSA-PKCS1-v1_5'` (that is, PKCS#1 v1.5 for signing) or `'RSA-PSS'`, depending on the padding scheme you want to use (for an explanation of these, please refer to *Chapter 6, Digital Signatures with Node.js and Trust*).

   The `modulusLength` property is the size of the key in bits, usually `2048`, `3072`, or `4096`.

For `publicExponent`, you should normally use this static value (equivalent to the number 65537, which is conventionally used with most implementations leveraging RSA), unless you have a reason to do otherwise:

```
new Uint8Array([1, 0, 1])
```

Finally, `hash` determines the hashing function to use and can be one of `'SHA-256'`, `'SHA-384'`, `'SHA-512'`, or `'SHA-1'` (this last value is not recommended as it's not secure, though it's available for compatibility reasons).

- Lastly, for **Elliptic Curve Cryptography**, use an object containing two properties: {`name, namedCurve`}.

  `name` is a string that can be either `'ECDH'` or `'ECDSA'`, respectively, if the generated key is to be used for ECDH key agreements (see *Chapter 5, Using Asymmetric and Hybrid Encryption in Node.js*) or for ECDSA digital signatures (see *Chapter 6, Digital Signatures with Node.js and Trust*).

  The `namedCurve` property, on the other hand, is the name of the curve to use. For the prime256v1 key, set this to `'P-256'` (how that curve is named in the NIST's specifications).

The `generateKey` function returns (asynchronously, via a promise) a `CryptoKey` object for AES keys. For asymmetric ciphers, it returns (a promise that resolves with) a dictionary containing {`privateKey, publicKey`}, both of which are `CryptoKey` objects.

Here are some examples of generating keys:

7.1: Generating an AES-256-GCM key for encryption and decryption:

```
const key = await window.crypto.subtle.generateKey(
    {
        name: 'AES-GCM',
        length: 256
    },
    true,
    ['encrypt', 'decrypt']
)
console.log(key) // CryptoKey object
```

7.2: Generating a 4,096-bit RSA-PSS key pair for signing and verifying signatures:

```
const keyPair = await window.crypto.subtle.generateKey(
    {
        name: 'RSA-PSS',
        modulusLength: 4096,
        publicExponent: new Uint8Array([1, 0, 1]),
        hash: 'SHA-256'
    },
    true,
    ['sign', 'verify']
)
console.log(keyPair.privateKey) // CryptoKey object
console.log(keyPair.publicKey) // CryptoKey object
```

7.3: Generating a P-256 elliptic curve key pair for an ECDH key derivation:

```
const keyPair = await window.crypto.subtle.generateKey(
    {
        name: 'ECDH',
        namedCurve: 'P-256'
    },
    false,
    ['deriveKey']
)
console.log(keyPair.privateKey) // CryptoKey object
console.log(keyPair.publicKey) // CryptoKey object
```

SubtleCrypto and Long-Running Operations

All the methods in the SubtleCrypto class (of which window.crypto.subtle is an instance) are asynchronous because they are executed in a background thread in the web browser. Because of that, they're also non-blocking (they do not block the main event loop of your JavaScript application), so it's not necessary to run them in a Web Worker, even when you're running intensive operations, such as generating large RSA key pairs.

Importing keys

The `generateKey` method we just saw generates a new, random key. If you want to simply reuse an existing key, you need to import it using the `crypto.subtle.importKey()` method.

The signature of the `importKey` method is as follows:

```
const keyPromise = window.crypto.subtle.importKey(
    format, data, algorithm, extractable, usages
)
```

Just like `generateKey`, this method returns a promise that resolves with a `CryptoKey` object containing the imported key. Unlike `generateKey`, however, this always returns a single key of the type that was imported: secret for symmetric keys, and either private or public for asymmetric ones.

The parameters are as follows:

- `format` is a string with the format of the key.

  For symmetric keys, set this to `'raw'` to import the key's data as-is.

  For asymmetric keys, use `'pkcs8'` for private keys (in PKCS#8 format) and `'spki'` for public ones (in SPKI/PKIX format), both DER-encoded – examples will be shown shortly. For more information on the formats for asymmetric keys, please refer to *Chapter 5, Using Asymmetric and Hybrid Encryption in Node.js*. Also, note that the Web Crypto APIs currently do not support keys in the older PKCS#1 format.

- `data` is an `ArrayBuffer` object or a typed array containing the key's data.

- The last three parameters (`algorithm`, `extractable`, `usages`) are the same as the ones we saw in the `generateKey` method.

Importing symmetric keys

To import a symmetric key, make sure that the key's bytes are in an `ArrayBuffer` object or a typed array, and set the format parameter to `'raw'`. You must also provide the correct value for `algorithm`. For example, to import a 256-bit key for use with AES-CBC, use the following sample code:

7.4: Importing a 256-bit AES-CBC key

```
const keyData = ... /* Key data goes here */
const key = await window.crypto.subtle.importKey(
```

```
    'raw',
    keyData,
    {
        name: 'AES-CBC',
        length: 256
    },
    false,
    ['encrypt', 'decrypt']
)
console.log(key) // CryptoKey object
```

The key's data is in the `keyData` variable, which needs to be an `ArrayBuffer` object or a typed array. Obtaining the key depends on your application: for example, it could be retrieved from a remote server or from `localStorage`. In many of those cases, the key is likely stored in base64-encoded format and needs to be decoded first.

Importing private and public keys

As we mentioned previously, the `importKey` method supports importing asymmetric keys, both private and public, in the PKCS#8 and SPKI formats, respectively, both of which are DER-encoded.

In *Chapter 5, Using Asymmetric and Hybrid Encryption in Node.js*, we mentioned that both those formats – PKCS#8 and SPKI – are encoded as DER and then normally stored in PEM files.

For example, the following is a P-256 (or prime256v1) private key encoded in a PEM block (part of the key was truncated for brevity):

```
-----BEGIN PRIVATE KEY-----
MIGHAgEAMBMGByqGSM49AgEGCCqGSM49AwEHBG0wawIBAQ [...]
lrYpXDlESMqGL0jDalMGiX9bVM71Pnm
-----END PRIVATE KEY-----
```

As we saw earlier, Node.js supports importing these keys as-is, as whole PEM files. Web Crypto, on the other hand, requires us to manually extract the DER-encoded bytes from the PEM document.

To do that, with both private and public keys, we need to do the following:

1. First, remove the PEM header and footer; that is, `-----BEGIN FOO-----` and `-----END FOO-----`.

2. Decode the key from base64 to obtain the raw DER-encoded byte sequence.

Here's a sample function that imports a public or private key from PEM:

7.5: Importing public and private keys from PEM (key-from-pem.js)

```
import {Decode} from 'arraybuffer-encoding/base64/standard'
function keyFromPem(keyType, pem, algorithm, exportable,
    usages) {
  let format, header, footer
  switch (keyType) {
    case 'public':
        format = 'spki'
        header = '-----BEGIN PUBLIC KEY-----'
        footer = '-----END PUBLIC KEY-----'
        break
    case 'private':
        format = 'pkcs8'
        header = '-----BEGIN PRIVATE KEY-----'
        footer = '-----END PRIVATE KEY-----'
        break
  }
  const keyData = Decode(
      pem.trim()
        .slice(header.length, -1 * footer.length)
        .replaceAll('\n', '')
  )
  return crypto.subtle.importKey(format, keyData, algorithm,
      exportable, usages)
}
```

This code depends on a base64 decoding library that returns a typed array or
ArrayBuffer; we used arraybuffer-encoding from npm in this example.

The keyFromPem function returns a promise that resolves with a CryptoKey object
containing the key that was read from a PEM document. It accepts five parameters:

- keyType is a string that is either 'public' or 'private', determining the
  key type.

- pem is the PEM-encoded key, as a string.

- The remaining parameters (algorithm, exportable, usages) are the same as
  in the generateKey and importKey methods.

The body of the function implements the algorithm described previously.

You can find the full code for this function (with comments and some more error handling), as well as an example of how to use it, in this book's GitHub repository, in the `key-from-pem.js` file in the `ch7-ch8-browser-cryptography` folder.

Exporting keys

The last Web Crypto API we'll be analyzing in this chapter is `crypto.subtle.exportKey()`, which allows us to export the key that's stored in a `CryptoKey` object. For example, after generating a new key, it's common to export it to a variable and then store it somewhere (in `localStorage`, on a remote server, and so on).

`exportKey` returns the key's data as-is, without any encryption or wrapping, so you should treat the exported key material with care. As we mentioned earlier, for security reasons only keys that were created with the `exportable` flag set to `true` can be exported.

The signature of the method is as follows:

```
window.crypto.subtle.exportKey(format, key)
```

- The `format` parameter is one of `'raw'`, `'pkcs8'`, or `'spki'`, which have the same meaning we saw with the `importKey` function: they're used for secret/symmetric, private, and public keys, respectively.

- The `key` parameter contains the `CryptoKey` object that you want to export. The function returns a promise that resolves with the key in an `ArrayBuffer` object.

If your `CryptoKey` object contains a **symmetric** key, such as an AES key, the result of the `exportKey` function is (a promise that resolves to) an `ArrayBuffer` object containing your key's bytes. Besides optionally encoding the data to base64 or hex before storing it, no further processing is necessary.

Exporting asymmetric keys

When you're using `exportKey` with a `CryptoKey` object containing an asymmetric key, either public or private, the result is the DER-encoded byte sequence of the key. This is the same data format that the `importKey` method accepts as input.

In most cases, and for compatibility with other applications, it's convenient to encode those keys in PEM format, and doing so requires performing the actions we've explained for `importKey` in reverse:

1. Encode the key's data (the DER-encoded byte sequence) into base64, adding a line break every 64 characters.

2. Add the PEM header and footer; that is, `-----BEGIN FOO-----` and `-----END FOO-----`.

Here's a sample function that allows us to export a public or private key to PEM:

7.6: Exporting public and private keys to PEM (pem-from-key.js)

```js
import {Encode} from 'arraybuffer-encoding/base64/standard'
async function pemFromKey(keyType, key) {
    let format, header, footer
    switch (keyType) {
        case 'public':
            format = 'spki'
            header = '-----BEGIN PUBLIC KEY-----'
            footer = '-----END PUBLIC KEY-----'
            break
        case 'private':
            format = 'pkcs8'
            header = '-----BEGIN PRIVATE KEY-----'
            footer = '-----END PRIVATE KEY-----'
            break
    }
    const keyData = await crypto.subtle.exportKey(format, key)
    const pem = [
        header,
        Encode(keyData).replace(/(.{64})/g, '$1\n'),
        footer
    ].join('\n')
    return pem
}
```

Like the `keyFromPem` method we saw earlier, this function accepts a `keyType` parameter that is a string with a value of either `'public'` or `'private'`, depending on the type of key to export. It also takes the `CryptoKey` object in the second parameter, `key`. The method is asynchronous and returns a promise that resolves with a string with the PEM-encoded key.

The body of the function implements the algorithm described previously, relying on a base64-encoding library to convert from an `ArrayBuffer` into base64: in this example, we've used the `arraybuffer-encoding` package from npm.

In the function's body, the `replace` function (highlighted) is used as a quirky one-liner to add a newline after every 64 characters in the base64-encoded data; while I am normally not a fan of "clever" solutions like these that are hard to read, I hope you will forgive me this time as I didn't want to add many lines of code that could have been clearer but are irrelevant for our goals.

You can find the full code for this function (with comments and some more error handling), and an example of how to use it, in this book's GitHub repository, in the `pem-from-key.js` file in the `ch7-ch8-browser-cryptography` folder.

Summary

In this chapter, we started looking into performing cryptographic operations in the web browser using frontend JavaScript code. Doing this allows us to build more kinds of applications, such as those using end-to-end encryption, but it also comes with other challenges and security risks, including some that are unique to code that runs in a web browser.

We then started looking at some "core" concepts for using cryptography in the browser, including dealing with binary data, using base64 and hex encoding, and working with keys: generating, importing, and exporting them.

In the next chapter, we'll continue exploring how to perform cryptography in the browser by completing our overview of the Web Crypto APIs, plus more.

8

Performing Common Cryptographic Operations in the Browser

In the previous chapter, we introduced the idea of performing cryptographic operations in the browser, and we looked at some core concepts, such as how to manage binary data in client-side JavaScript and how to create, import, and export keys with `CryptoKey` objects.

We'll cover the rest of the topics in this chapter by looking at how to perform the cryptographic operations we learned about in *Part 2* of this book, this time within the web browser: hashing, symmetric encryption, asymmetric and hybrid encryption, and digital signatures.

Please note that we won't be explaining what each cryptographic operation does or when you should use which in this chapter. Because of that, I recommend that you familiarize yourself with the various operations first, reviewing *Chapter 3, File and Password Hashing with Node.js* to *Chapter 6, Digital Signatures with Node.js and Trust,* if needed.

Lastly, fasten your seatbelts, as we'll be moving fast in the next few pages while covering the following topics:

- Hashing with SHA using the WebCrypto APIs, and key derivation and password hashing with Argon2 in the browser

- Symmetric encryption in the browser with AES and the WebCrypto APIs

- Asymmetric and hybrid encryption with the WebCrypto APIs, using RSA and ECDH

- Calculating and verifying digital signatures using RSA and ECDSA with the WebCrypto APIs

Technical requirements

Please refer to the *Technical requirements* section of *Chapter 7, Introduction to Cryptography in the Browser*, since the technical requirements are the same for this chapter too.

In particular, please note that all the samples in this chapter have been optimized so that they can be included in modern browser-based applications that are packaged using a bundler for JavaScript code, such as Webpack or similar. Alternatively, the code can also be executed in Node.js 15 or higher by importing the compatibility object from the `crypto` package.

To make it easier to experiment with the code shown in this chapter, we've created a "playground" that you can run within your web browser: `https://bit.ly/crypto-playground`.

As a reminder, all the code samples for this chapter and the previous can be found in this book's GitHub repository at `https://bit.ly/crypto-ch8`.

Lastly, please note that some code samples depend on libraries to convert from buffers (such as `ArrayBuffer` objects or its views) into base64-encoded or hex-encoded strings, or vice versa. As we mentioned in the previous chapter, these routines are not built into the Web Platform, so we need to rely on external libraries instead. While any suitable module from npm will do the job (and we recommended a few in the previous chapter), in these examples we'll be using `arraybuffer-encoding` (`https://www.npmjs.com/package/arraybuffer-encoding`).

Hashing and key derivation

Hashing was the first operation we covered in this book, in *Chapter 3, File and Password Hashing with Node.js*. As you will recall, hashing functions can be used for a variety of purposes, including the following:

- Calculating the checksum (or digest) of a document or file. For this specific scenario, we recommended the use of the **SHA-2** family of hashes (including SHA-256, SHA-384, and SHA-512).

- Hashing passwords before they're stored in a database. In this case, we recommended using algorithms in the **Argon2** suite or **scrypt**.

- Deriving symmetric encryption keys from low-entropy inputs such as passphrases, as we saw in *Chapter 4, Symmetric Encryption in Node.js*. For this scenario, we once again recommended using **Argon2** or **scrypt**.

Support for calculating digests with SHA-2 is built into the Web Platform, and at the time of writing, it is one of the only two hashing algorithms that have been standardized and are available in all browsers (the other one is SHA-1, which, as we've seen, is considered broken and deprecated, and should only be used for compatibility reasons).

Neither Argon2 nor scrypt are available in the Web Platform, so we'll need to rely on external modules, such as the `hash-wasm` package from npm (`https://www.npmjs.com/package/hash-wasm`); this specific library was selected because it uses fast WebAssembly binaries. In this chapter, we'll see code samples for Argon2, but the same package contains routines for scrypt as well.

Calculating checksums

We can use the `crypto.subtle.digest()` method to calculate a SHA-2 hash, as follows:

8.1: Calculating the checksum of a message with SHA-256 (hash-sha256.js)

```
import {Encode} from 'arraybuffer-encoding/hex'
;(async () => {
    const message = (new TextEncoder())
        .encode('Hello world!')
    const result = await window.crypto.subtle.digest(
        'SHA-256',
```

```
        message,
    )
    console.log(Encode(result))
}) ()
```

The previous code (which, as usual, is wrapped in an **Immediately-Invoked Function Expression (IIFE)** so that it can be used the await expression) takes a string message, converts it into a buffer with TextEncoder (as explained in the previous chapter), and then calculates its SHA-256 digest. Eventually, the result is printed to the console, hex-encoded.

The crypto.subtle.digest(algorithm, data) method accepts two arguments:

- algorithm is the name of hashing algorithm to use, which is a string with a value of 'SHA-256', 'SHA-384', or 'SHA-512'. It's also possible to use 'SHA-1', but that is not secure and should only be used for compatibility with older systems.

- data is the message to digest, as an ArrayBuffer or one of its views (such as Uint8Array).

The result is a promise that resolves with an ArrayBuffer containing the digest.

Streaming Support

At the time of writing, the WebCrypto APIs do not include support for streams, neither for hashing nor for working with encryption or digital signatures. This makes using the methods presented in this chapter not always practical when dealing with large files.

If your web-based application requires dealing with documents that are too large to be kept in memory, you will need to look into third-party modules from npm (for hashing, this includes hash-wasm, which we'll encounter in the next section). Alternatively, you can build a chunking mechanism, where data is hashed or encrypted in fixed-length chunks. One example is the "DARE" format, which was created by the engineers at MinIO: https://bit.ly/crypto-dare.

Hashing passwords

Using the routines from the `hash-wasm` module from npm, we can calculate the hash of a password using the `argon2d`, `argon2i`, and `argon2id` functions that it exports. Additionally, it's possible to verify that a password that's been submitted by the user matches the hash stored in a database with the `argon2Verify` method from the same library.

Please refer to *Chapter 3, File and Password Hashing with Node.js*, for a recap on Argon2, its details, and its variants:

8.2: Hashing passwords with Argon2 (hash-argon2.js)

```js
import {argon2id, argon2Verify} from 'hash-wasm'
;(async () => {
    const passphrase = 'correct horse battery staple'
    const salt = new Uint8Array(16)
    window.crypto.getRandomValues(salt)
    const hash = await argon2id({
        outputType: 'encoded',
        password: passphrase,
        salt: salt,
        hashLength: 32,
        parallelism: 1,
        iterations: 3,
        memorySize: 4096,
    })
    console.log('Hash:', hash)

    const isValid = await argon2Verify({
        password: passphrase,
        hash: hash
    })
    console.log('Is valid?', isValid)
})()
```

The previous code takes a passphrase (in this case, hardcoded in the `passphrase` variable) and calculates its hash with Argon2 in the `argon2id` variant. The `argon2id` function accepts a dictionary with several parameters:

- When hashing passwords to store the hash in a database, you want to set `outputType` to `'encoded'`. Just like we saw in *Chapter 3, File and Password Hashing with Node.js*, this makes the result a string that contains, in addition to the hash, the salt and all the tuning options that were used for Argon2, making it easier to verify the hash later.

- The password/passphrase is passed to the `password` key.

- We also need to pass to the method a random `salt`, which we're generating before invoking the function.

- With `hashLength`, we can configure the number of bytes to return; that is, how long the hash should be. A value of `32` is a sensible default for password hashing.

- Lastly, `parallelism`, `iteration`, and `memorySize` (in KB) control the "cost" of the Argon2 invocation. Higher values will require more time and/or memory. You can refer to the discussion in *Chapter 4, Symmetric Encryption in Node.js*, for more details on these parameters and how they can be tuned.

The function returns a promise that resolves with a string when `outputType` is `'encoded'`. The computed hash can be stored in a database and retrieved later.

When a user types the password again, you can verify that it matches the hash with the `argon2Verify` method, as shown in the preceding example. This function accepts a dictionary with two keys:

- `password` is the password/passphrase the user just typed. The method will check if it matches the one that was used when the hash was created.

- `hash` is the hash of the password, as a string in "encoded" form with all the parameters included.

The result is a promise that resolves with a value of `true` if the password matches the value in the hash.

The previous code sample will print something like this in the console (the actual output will be different every time because of the random salt):

```
Hash:
$argon2id$v=19$m=4096,t=3,p=1$iSuXUkWhJ9343KE0W9BegA$dL83T-
LLTij9wLnfJXCTnF0IAMPvgXR3VSIefINM78vs
Is valid? True
```

Note that the hash in "encoded" mode contains all the parameters that were used to compute it, which are needed to verify that a password matches the hash.

Deriving encryption keys

We can use Argon2 to derive symmetric encryption keys by stretching passphrases, as we saw in *Chapter 4, Symmetric Encryption in Node.js*. The following is an example:

8.3: Deriving encryption keys with Argon2 (key-derivation-argon2.js)

```
import {argon2id} from 'hash-wasm'
;(async () => {
    const passphrase = 'correct horse battery staple'
    const salt = new Uint8Array(16)
    window.crypto.getRandomValues(salt)
    const rawKey = await argon2id({
        outputType: 'binary',
        password: passphrase,
        salt: salt,
        hashLength: 32,
        parallelism: 1,
        iterations: 3,
        memorySize: 4096,
    })
```

```
const key = await window.crypto.subtle.importKey(
    'raw', rawKey,
    'AES-GCM', false, ['encrypt', 'decrypt']
)
}) ()
```

In this example, we're once again using the `argon2id` method, but this time we're setting `outputType` to `'binary'`. This will make the function return a promise that resolves with an `ArrayBuffer` containing the raw encryption key, with as many bytes as requested with the `hashLength` option (in the preceding example, we're requesting a 256-bit, or 32-byte, key).

For us to be able to use the derived key as a symmetric encryption key (such as for AES-GCM), we need to import that in a `CryptoKey` object using the `crypto.subtle.importKey` method, as we saw in *Chapter 7, Introduction to Cryptography in the Browser*.

The `key` object can then be used to encrypt and decrypt data with AES, as we'll see in the next section.

Symmetric encryption

We first encountered symmetric encryption in *Chapter 4, Symmetric Encryption in Node.js*, where we covered two ciphers: **AES** and **ChaCha20-Poly1305**.

In this chapter, we'll focus solely on AES, given that it's the only symmetric cipher that's standardized in the WebCrypto APIs and available on all browsers, with a few different modes of operation. We'll look at encrypting and decrypting data using AES-GCM and AES-CBC, and then we'll use AES-KW (RFC 3394) for wrapping and unwrapping keys.

While we won't cover ChaCha20-Poly1305, you can find several packages on `npm` that offer support for that, including implementations in pure JavaScript or that leverage native code via WebAssembly.

Encrypting and decrypting messages with AES

The WebCrypto APIs include two methods for encrypting and decrypting data:

- `crypto.subtle.encrypt(algorithm, key, data)`
- `crypto.subtle.decrypt(algorithm, key, data)`

Both methods have similar parameters:

- `algorithm` is an object that contains two keys: the `name` property of the algorithm and its `iv`.

- `key` is a `CryptoKey` object containing a symmetric key for the algorithm that you want to use.

- `data` is the plaintext (for `encrypt`) or ciphertext (for `decrypt`), and it's a buffer or buffer-like object in both cases.

Using AES-CBC and AES-GCM

Let's look at an example of using AES-CBC to encrypt data (note that this is a snippet that uses the `await` keyword, so it should be placed inside an `async` function):

8.4: Encrypting data with AES-256-CBC (part of symmetric-aes-cbc.js)

```
const plaintext = (new TextEncoder()).encode('Hello world!')
const key = await window.crypto.subtle.generateKey(
    {name: 'AES-CBC', length: 256},
    false, ['encrypt', 'decrypt']
)
const iv = new Uint8Array(16)
window.crypto.getRandomValues(iv)
const encrypted = await window.crypto.subtle.encrypt(
    {name: 'AES-CBC', iv: iv}, key, plaintext
)
const encryptedStore = new Uint8Array([
    iv,
    new Uint8Array(encrypted)
])
console.log('encryptedStore:', encryptedStore)
```

This snippet recreates the same behavior as the code we saw in *Chapter 4, Symmetric Encryption in Node.js*, but this time it's using the WebCrypto APIs. Let's look at it in more detail:

1. As we saw regarding hashing in the previous section, if we're trying to encrypt a string, we need to encode that as a `Uint8Array` using `TextEncoder`.

2. We must then generate a new 256-bit key for use with AES-CBC with the `crypto.subtle.generateKey` method, as we saw in *Chapter 7, Introduction to Cryptography in the Browser*. We make the key non-extractable (passing `false` as the second argument) and specify that it can be used to encrypt and decrypt data (with the list of strings in the third argument).

3. We then proceed to generate a random IV using the `crypto.getRandomValues` method with a `Uint8Array` with a size of 16 bytes. This method has the effect of filling the array with random numbers.

   As we discussed in the previous chapter, `crypto.getRandomValues` does not offer a random generator with high entropy, so we shouldn't use that to generate cryptographic keys; however, it's considered acceptable for generating IVs, as in this case.

4. Next, we must use the `crypto.subtle.encrypt` method (asynchronously) to encrypt our buffer. The object that's passed as the first argument, `algorithm`, contains two keys.

   The `name` property is set to AES-CBC, specifying the cipher to use and the mode of operation.

   The `iv` property contains the buffer containing the random IV that we just generated.

   Note that we're not passing the size of the key, which is inferred from the `key` object, which is passed as the second argument.

5. The last step involves concatenating the IV and the ciphertext. As we saw in *Chapter 4, Symmetric Encryption in Node.js*, it's common practice to store or transmit the two together, as a single byte sequence with the IV at the beginning of the message.

To decrypt the message, we can reverse the operations by using the data from `encryptedStore` we computed previously and the same `key` object:

8.5: Decrypting data with AES-256-CBC (part of symmetric-aes-cbc.js)

```
const iv = encryptedStore.slice(0, 16)
const encrypted = encryptedStore.slice(16)
const decrypted = await window.crypto.subtle.decrypt(
    {name: 'AES-CBC', iv: iv}, key, encrypted
)
const plaintext = (new TextDecoder('utf-8')).decode(decrypted)
console.log('decrypted:', plaintext)
```

To start, we slice the `encryptedStore` buffer and extract the first 16 bytes, which are our IV. The remaining part of the buffer (from the byte in position 16 onwards) is used as the ciphertext.

We then use the `crypto.subtle.decrypt` method to perform the decryption. For the first parameter, `algorithm`, we're passing an object that contains the same properties (and same values) that we used when encrypting the message.

Because the method returns an `ArrayBuffer` object, we need to use a `TextDecoder` to convert it into a UTF-8 string and print the message in cleartext again.

The full code sample can be found in this book's GitHub repository, in the `symmetric-aes-256-cbc.js` file in the `ch7-ch8-browser-cryptography` folder.

In the same folder, you can also find an example of using AES-GCM, in the `symmetric-aes-256-gcm.js` file.

As you may recall, AES-GCM is an authenticated cipher that offers a guarantee of integrity in addition to confidentiality. In GCM mode, the result of `crypto.subtle.encrypt` has the authentication tag automatically appended at the end of the ciphertext, which `crypto.subtle.decrypt` knows to extract and compare when decrypting data.

Because of that, using AES-GCM with the WebCrypto APIs is as simple as replacing all instances of `'AES-CBC'` with `'AES-GCM'` in the code; no further changes are required.

Using AES-KW

We first encountered AES-KW in *Chapter 4, Symmetric Encryption in Node.js*, and explained it's a special mode of operation that's defined in RFC 3394 that is optimized for wrapping and unwrapping (encrypting and decrypting) other symmetric keys that are up to 256 bits in length.

AES-KW is available as a built-in algorithm that can be used with the `crypto.subtle.wrap()` method. Compared to the implementation available in Node.js, we don't need to set the IV to the static value described by RFC 3394, as that is done automatically for us.

Let's look at an example. Let's assume we have two keys: a `symmetricKey` that is randomly generated and that we'll use to encrypt our data (for example, to encrypt a message or a file), and a `wrappingKey` that is derived from a passphrase (for example, using Argon2). In the following snippet, we're defining both variables:

```
const wrappingKey = await deriveKey(passphrase, salt)
const symmetricKey = await window.crypto.subtle.generateKey(
    {name: 'AES-CBC', length: 256}, true,
    ['encrypt', 'decrypt']
)
```

- `wrappingKey` is returned by a `deriveKey()` function that you define: for example, it could be a function that uses Argon2 to derive a `CryptoKey` object from a passphrase and salt (this is implemented in full in the complete example file on GitHub). Regardless of how you derive the wrapping key, two things must be set when you're creating/deriving the `CryptoKey` object: the algorithm must be `'AES-KW'`, and the usages must include `['wrapKey', 'unwrapKey']`.

- `symmetricKey` is a randomly generated AES-CBC key. We can use AES-KW to wrap any kind of symmetric key, so long as it's 256-bit long or less (assuming the wrapping key is 256-bit itself). What matters is that this `CryptoKey` object must have the exportable flag set to `true`; otherwise, the key wrapping will fail with an error (keys that can't be exported cannot be wrapped either).

With `wrappingKey` and `symmetricKey` defined for both `CryptoKey` instances, we can proceed to wrap and unwrap the key:

8.6: Wrapping and unwrapping keys with AES-KW (part of symmetric-aes-kw.js)

```
const wrappedKey = await window.crypto.subtle.wrapKey(
    'raw', symmetricKey, wrappingKey, {name: 'AES-KW'}
)
console.log({wrappedKey})


const unwrappedKey = await window.crypto.subtle.unwrapKey(
    'raw', wrappedKey, wrappingKey, {name: 'AES-KW'},
    {name: 'AES-CBC'}, false, ['encrypt', 'decrypt']
)
console.log({unwrappedKey})
```

The first part of the sample wraps the key using `crypto.subtle.wrap()`. This method takes four arguments:

1. The format, which is always the `'raw'` string for symmetric keys.

2. The key to wrap as a `CryptoKey` object: in our example, that's the `symmetricKey` variable. As we've seen, this key must be exportable.

3. The wrapping key, again as a `CryptoKey` object. In our case, that's `wrappingKey`. As a reminder, this key's algorithm must be `'AES-KW'` and the key must have `'wrapKey'` as allowed usage.

4. The key wrapping algorithm to use – in this case, an object that contains a `name` property with a value of `'AES-KW'`.

This function returns a promise that resolves with a buffer containing the wrapped key. After optionally encoding it to hex or base64, that key can be stored or transmitted as appropriate (for example, stored in `localStorage` or transmitted to a remote server to be archived there).

Unwrapping the key requires using the `crypto.subtle.unwrap()` method, which requires a very long list of parameters. The first four are symmetrical to the ones that are used by `crypto.subtle.wrap()`:

- The format of the key to import, which is always `'raw'`.

- The wrapped (encrypted) key as a buffer. This is the same value that was returned by `crypto.subtle.wrap()`.

- The wrapping key, as a `CryptoKey` object, which in our example is `wrappingKey`. This object must have the `'AES-KW'` algorithm and `'unwrapKey'` as its allowed usage.

- The key wrapping algorithm to use, which is the same value we used previously; that is, `{name: 'AES-KW'}`.

The last three arguments are used to specify the properties of the resulting `CryptoKey` object (returned asynchronously, as the result of a promise) and define what the unwrapped key can be used for: the algorithm the key is used for, whether it's exportable, and its intended usages. These are the same parameters that we've passed to methods such as `crypto.subtle.generateKey()`.

These examples are all that we had to cover with regards to symmetric ciphers. In the next section, we're going to look at asymmetric and hybrid cryptography in the browser.

Asymmetric and hybrid cryptography

In *Chapter 5, Using Asymmetric and Hybrid Encryption in Node.js*, we explained how asymmetric cryptography differs from symmetric (or shared key), and we looked at various examples of using asymmetric ciphers for encrypting data, performing key agreements, and building hybrid encryption schemes. In this section, we'll build upon what we learned in that chapter and show examples of using the same algorithms in a web browser, using the WebCrypto APIs.

Encrypting and decrypting short messages with RSA

RSA is the first asymmetric cipher we encountered in *Chapter 5, Using Asymmetric and Hybrid Encryption in Node.js*.

When using RSA, each party has a key pair consisting of a private key and a public one. As we've explained, messages are encrypted with a public key (which can be distributed with the world safely) and decrypted using the corresponding private key (which must be kept highly protected).

As we saw in *Chapter 7, Introduction to Cryptography in the Browser*, you can generate an RSA key pair using `crypto.subtle.generateKey()`, like so:

8.7: Generating an RSA-OAEP key pair (part of asymmetric-rsa.js)

```
const keyPair = await window.crypto.subtle.generateKey(
    {
        name: 'RSA-OAEP',
        modulusLength: 2048,
        publicExponent: new Uint8Array([0x01, 0x00, 0x01]),
        hash: 'SHA-256'
    },
    false, ['encrypt', 'decrypt']
)
console.log(keyPair.publicKey, keyPair.privateKey)
```

The preceding snippet generates a `keyPair` object that contains two properties, each a `CryptoKey` object: `keyPair.publicKey` and `keyPair.privateKey`.

This code is very similar to what we saw in the previous examples to generate symmetric keys, and we explained this in detail in *Chapter 7, Introduction to Cryptography in the Browser* (see the *Generating keys* section). It's worth recalling that the first argument that's passed to `generateKey` is a dictionary that specifies the properties of the key. In this case, we're doing the following:

- We're creating an RSA key that will be used for encrypting and decrypting data with the **RSA-OAEP** padding (using the `name` property) and SHA-256 for hashing (set with the `hash` property). The WebCrypto APIs only support OAEP padding (officially, PKCS#1 v2 padding) and do not implement the legacy PKCS#1 v1.5 padding, which is considered insecure.

  For a refresher of the various padding schemes, you can refer to the *Using RSA for encryption and decryption* section in *Chapter 5, Using Asymmetric and Hybrid Encryption in Node.js*.

- The size of the key in bits is specified in the `modulusLength` property, and in this case, it is `2048`. Other common values include `3072` and `4096`.

- For `publicExponent`, you should normally use the following static value (equivalent to the decimal 65537):

```
new Uint8Array([1, 0, 1])
```

- Lastly, we're using SHA-256 as the hashing algorithm with the `hash` property. Other algorithms are supported, including SHA-1, SHA-384, and SHA-512.

Once you've generated a key pair, you can use that to encrypt and decrypt messages with the `crypto.subtle.encrypt()` and `crypto.subtle.decrypt()` methods:

8.8: Encrypting and decrypting messages with RSA-OAEP (part of asymmetric-rsa.js)

```
const encrypted = await window.crypto.subtle.encrypt(
    {name: 'RSA-OAEP'}, keyPair.publicKey,
    plaintext // Plaintext message as buffer
)


const decrypted = await window.crypto.subtle.decrypt(
    {name: 'RSA-OAEP'}, keyPair.privateKey, encrypted
)
```

The previous snippet is almost the same as the code we saw for encrypting and decrypting data with AES. The only differences are passing `'RSA-OAEP'` as the name of the algorithm, and using the `publicKey` property of `keyPair` when encrypting and the `privateKey` property when decrypting.

The full code sample that shows how to encrypt (short) messages is available in the `asymmetric-rsa.js` file in this book's GitHub repository, in the `ch7-ch8-browser-cryptography` folder.

Hybrid encryption with RSA and AES

As you may recall from *Chapter 5, Using Asymmetric and Hybrid Encryption in Node.js*, asymmetric ciphers such as RSA can only encrypt small amounts of data and are particularly slow. For example, with OAEP padding and SHA-256 as hashing (as we saw in the previous section), RSA can only encrypt 190 bytes! (Trying to encrypt longer messages with the WebCrypto APIs will throw a runtime exception.)

Applications that need to encrypt messages of an arbitrary length (including files), then, leverage hybrid encryption schemes, where the message is encrypted with AES using a random key, and the key is then wrapped using RSA.

From a practical point of view, the implementation is very similar to the example we saw earlier in this chapter, where we used AES-KW to wrap a shared key, except this time, the key wrapping is done with an asymmetric algorithm.

The following snippet generates a random AES-256-GCM key that can be used to encrypt and decrypt data, generates an RSA-4096 key pair for wrapping and unwrapping the key, and then shows you how to use the `crypto.subtle.wrapKey()` and `crypto.subtle.unwrapKey()` to wrap and unwrap the symmetric key, respectively. You may notice that it has many similarities to *Sample 8.6*, where we used AES-KW instead:

8.9: Wrapping an AES key using RSA

```
const symmetricKey = await window.crypto.subtle.generateKey(
    {name: 'AES-GCM', length: 256}, true,
    ['encrypt', 'decrypt']
)
const rsaKeyPair = await window.crypto.subtle.generateKey(
    {
        name: 'RSA-OAEP', modulusLength: 4096,
        hash: 'SHA-256',
        publicExponent: new Uint8Array([0x01, 0x00, 0x01])
    },
    false, ['wrapKey', 'unwrapKey']
)
const wrappedKey = await window.crypto.subtle.wrapKey(
    'raw', symmetricKey,
    rsaKeyPair.publicKey, {name: 'RSA-OAEP'}
)
const unwrappedKey = await window.crypto.subtle.unwrapKey(
    'raw', wrappedKey,
    rsaKeyPair.privateKey, {name: 'RSA-OAEP'},
    {name: 'AES-GCM'}, false, ['decrypt']
)
```

These few lines allow you to wrap and unwrap symmetric AES keys, which can then be used to encrypt messages and implement hybrid encryption schemes. For the sake of brevity, we won't be including the full source code here; we will point you to this book's GitHub repository instead. In the `hybrid-rsa.js` file in the `ch7-ch8-browser-cryptography` folder, you can find a full, extensively commented implementation of a hybrid encryption scheme that uses AES-GCM with random keys to encrypt and decrypt files, where the keys are then wrapped with RSA.

Using elliptic curves for ECDH key agreements and ECIES hybrid encryption

The second part of *Chapter 5, Using Asymmetric and Hybrid Encryption in Node.js,* was dedicated to using elliptic-curve cryptography to implement key agreements using **Elliptic Curve Diffie-Hellman** (**ECDH**) and then using hybrid encryption schemes based on ECDH and AES. In the same chapter, we covered the benefits of using ECDH for a key agreement rather than wrapping keys with a cipher such as RSA.

Performing an ECDH key agreement

As we saw in the previous chapter, we can generate a key pair for ECDH with a function like this:

8.10: Creating a new key pair for ECDH (part of key-exchange-ecdh.js)

```
function newKeyPair() {
    return window.crypto.subtle.generateKey(
        {name: 'ECDH', namedCurve: 'P-256'},
        false, ['deriveKey']
    )
}
```

We should highlight two things in this code sample:

- The dictionary that contains the algorithm's properties contains two keys: name, which is the name of the algorithm, which should always be 'ECDH' in this case, and namedCurve, which contains the identifier of the elliptic curve to use, with the names that were assigned by the NIST.

As we saw in *Chapter 7, Introduction to Cryptography in the Browser* (in the *Generating keys* section), the WebCrypto APIs only have standardized support for the three most common NIST curves, which include `'P-256'` (we referred to this curve as prime256v1 in Node.js, which is sometimes called secp256r1) and the longer `'P-384'` and `'P-512'`. Other curves, such as the increasingly popular Curve25519 which we encountered in *Chapter 5, Using Asymmetric and Hybrid Encryption in Node.js* are not (yet) supported in the Web Platform. If your application requires that you use them in the browser, you will need to rely on third-party modules from npm.

- The key must be generated with `'deriveKey'` as an allowed usage.

To perform an ECDH key agreement, given a party's private key and another party's public key, we can use the `crypto.subtle.deriveKey()` method, as shown in this example:

8.11: Using crypto.subtle.deriveKey to perform an ECDH agreement (part of key-exchange-ecdh.js)

```
function deriveSecretKey(privateKey, publicKey) {
    return window.crypto.subtle.deriveKey(
        {
            name: 'ECDH',
            public: publicKey
        },
        privateKey,
        {name: 'AES-GCM', length: 256}, false, ['encrypt',
            'decrypt']
    )
}
```

The `deriveSecretKey()` method returns a promise that resolves with a `CryptoKey` object and allows you to perform an ECDH key agreement. It takes five arguments:

1. The first parameter is a dictionary that includes two properties: `name` (the algorithm's name), which is always `'ECDH'` in this case, and `public`, which contains the **second party's public key** object.

2. The second parameter is the **first party's private key** object.

3. The remaining three arguments are used to define the kind of key that is derived, whether it can be extracted, and the derived key's usages. These are the same arguments that we've passed to many other methods, including `crypto.subtle.generateKey()`.

With the `newKeyPair()` and `deriveSecretKey()` functions we just defined in *Sample 8.10* and *Sample 8.11*, we can demonstrate a key agreement between two parties (our usual friends, Alice and Bob), each one with a ECDH key pair:

8.12: Example of an ECDH agreement between Alice and Bob (part of key-exchange-ecdh.js)

```
const aliceKeyPair = await newKeyPair()
const bobKeyPair = await newKeyPair()
const aliceSharedKey = await deriveSecretKey(
    aliceKeyPair.privateKey,
    bobKeyPair.publicKey
)
const bobSharedKey = await deriveSecretKey(
    bobKeyPair.privateKey,
    aliceKeyPair.publicKey
)
```

In this example, after generating two key pairs, we're invoking `deriveSecretKey()` twice:

- The first time, we're invoking it as Alice would: with her private key and Bob's public key.

- The second time, we're invoking it as Bob would: with his private key and Alice's public key.

As we saw in *Chapter 5, Using Asymmetric and Hybrid Encryption in Node.js*, while learning about ECDH, the shared keys Alice and Bob generate are identical: `aliceSharedKey` and `bobSharedKey` contain the same AES-256-GCM key (technically, they're two different `CryptoKey` objects, but they are built from byte-for-byte identical keys).

> **Tip**
> Try running the previous code but make the keys exportable, then export them and compare their values for equivalence.

Stretching the keys derived with ECDH

While the code shown in the previous section is functional, as we learned in *Chapter 5, Using Asymmetric and Hybrid Encryption in Node.js*, the output of an ECDH agreement is not perfectly uniform, so those keys do not offer the best security right out of the box. Just like we did in that chapter, then, we should stretch the result of the ECDH agreement with a **Key Derivation Function (KDF)** to increase the entropy.

Any KDF will work, but for this specific use case, we don't need to get particularly fancy and a salted SHA-256 will be enough (as we did in the examples in *Chapter 5, Using Asymmetric and Hybrid Encryption in Node.js*).

The `crypto.subtle.deriveKey()` method we used just moments ago does not allow you to modify the derived key. Instead, we need to use the "lower-level" `crypto.subtle.deriveBits()` method and do a few more rounds of processing.

`deriveBits()` returns a promise that resolves with an `ArrayBuffer` (instead of a `CryptoKey` object, as in `deriveKey()`) and takes three arguments:

- The first two arguments are the same as in the `deriveKey()` method.
- The third argument is the number of bits that should be derived from the ECDH agreement, such as `256` for a 256-bit key.

Now, we can modify the `deriveSecretKey(privateKey, publicKey)` function we defined in *Sample 8.11* so that it looks like this:

8.13: The updated deriveSecretKey function, which uses a salted SHA-256 hash to stretch the result of the ECDH agreement (part of key-exchange-ecdh-sha256.js)

```
async function deriveSecretKey(privateKey, publicKey, salt) {
    // #1
    const ecdhResult = await window.crypto.subtle.deriveBits(
        {name: 'ECDH', public: publicKey}, privateKey, 256
    )
    // #2
    const base = new Uint8Array(
        [...new Uint8Array(ecdhResult), ...salt]
    )
    const rawKey = await window.crypto.subtle.digest('SHA-256',
        base)
    // #3
```

```
return window.crypto.subtle.importKey(
    'raw', rawKey,
    {name: 'AES-GCM'}, false, ['encrypt', 'decrypt']
)
}
```

To start, note that the updated `deriveSecretKey()` method accepts a third parameter, called `salt`, which is a buffer object that contains several random bytes (the amount of which is up to your discretion – it could be 16-bytes long, for example). Despite that, the type of the returned object doesn't change: it's still a (promise that resolves with a) `CryptoKey` object containing a shared key.

The preceding code can be divided into three parts:

1. The first few lines use the `crypto.subtle.deriveBits()` method to derive a buffer, in this case containing 256 bits of data (as per the last argument that was passed to it).

2. Next, we create a `Uint8Array` object that contains the concatenation of the result of the ECDH function and the salt (note that `ecdhResult` is an `ArrayBuffer` object, so we need to create a `Uint8Array` from it for the code to work). We then calculate the SHA-256 digest of this buffer: the result (which is 256 bits long) will be our shared key, in raw bytes form.

3. Lastly, we take the raw bytes that were generated by the hashing function and import them into a `CryptoKey` object using `crypto.subtle.importKey()`, as we've done many times before.

You can find the full example, showing the usage of the updated `deriveSecretKey()` function, in the `key-exchange-ecdh-sha256.js` file in this book's GitHub repository, again in the `ch7-ch8-browser-cryptography` folder.

Hybrid encryption with ECIES

Elliptic Curve Integrated Encryption Scheme (**ECIES**) is used to refer to hybrid encryption schemes that use ECDH to perform a key agreement and then encrypt data with a symmetric cipher (for example, AES-GCM). As we saw in *Chapter 5, Using Asymmetric and Hybrid Encryption in Node.js*, there isn't a single specification that defines how to adopt ECIES in a standard way, so each developer is free to choose any reasonable combination of algorithms as they see fit.

In this book's GitHub repository, you can find a full example of performing hybrid encryption with ECIES in the `hybrid-ecies.js` file, inside the `ch7-ch8-browser-cryptography` folder (the full code is too long to comfortably embed within these pages). This code sample, which is extensively commented, is nevertheless based on the `newKeyPair()` and `deriveSecretKey()` functions we analyzed previously in *Sample 8.10* and *Sample 8.13*, and it adds the code to encrypt and decrypt data using the derived secret key and a symmetric cipher.

In the code sample in `hybrid-ecies.js`, we are implementing an ECIES solution that uses the same algorithms as the one we implemented in *Chapter 5, Using Asymmetric and Hybrid Encryption in Node.js*:

- **Key agreement**: ECDH, using the P-256 curve

- **Key derivation function**: SHA-256 with a random, 16-byte salt

- **Symmetric encryption algorithm and Message Authentication Code**: AES-256-GCM

With this, we have covered everything in *Chapter 5, Using Asymmetric and Hybrid Encryption in Node.js*, which means we're ready to move on to the next – and last – topic: digital signatures.

Digital signatures

Digital signatures are the last class of cryptographic operations we learned about as we dedicated the biggest part of *Chapter 6, Digital Signatures with Node.js and Trust*, to them. Once again, in this section we'll revisit them by showing code samples that work in the browser using the WebCrypto APIs instead. Just as we did in *Chapter 6, Digital Signatures with Node.js and Trust*, we'll look at examples of calculating and verifying digital signatures using both RSA and ECDSA.

Digital signatures with the WebCrypto APIs

With the WebCrypto APIs, we can calculate a signature with the `crypto.subtle.sign(algorithm, key, data)` method. This returns a promise that resolves with an `ArrayBuffer` containing our signature's raw bytes, and it requires three parameters:

- `algorithm`, the first argument, is an object that contains options for the digital signature algorithm to use. We'll see the details of this in the following sections for the RSA and ECDSA signatures, respectively.

- `key` is the `CryptoKey` object containing the **private** part of the key. As a reminder, with digital signatures, you use the private part of the key to compute the signature, and the public part to verify it.

- `data` is the `ArrayBuffer` object or buffer view that contains the message to sign.

Likewise, to verify the signature, we can use the built-in `crypto.subtle.verify(algorithm, key, signature, data)` method. This returns a promise that resolves with a Boolean value that indicates whether the signature is valid. The arguments are as follows:

1. `algorithm` is a dictionary with the same options that were passed to the `crypto.subtle.sign()` method. We'll learn about this more in the next few pages.

2. `key` is the `CryptoKey` object containing the **public** part of the key.

3. `signature` is an `ArrayBuffer` or buffer view containing the raw bytes of the signature.

4. `data` is the `ArrayBuffer` object or buffer view containing the original message, against which the signature is checked.

Calculating and verifying RSA signatures

Support for RSA digital signatures is built into the WebCrypto APIs, with both the padding schemes we encountered in *Chapter 6, Digital Signatures with Node.js and Trust*: PKCS#1 v1.5 and PSS.

To generate a key pair, we can use the usual `crypto.subtle.generateKey()` method:

8.14: Generating an RSA key pair for digital signatures (part of sign-rsa.js)

```
const keyPair = await window.crypto.subtle.generateKey(
    {
        name: 'RSASSA-PKCS1-v1_5',
        modulusLength: 2048,
        publicExponent: new Uint8Array([0x01, 0x00, 0x01]),
        hash: 'SHA-256'
    },
    false, ['sign', 'verify']
)
const privateKey = keyPair.privateKey
const publicKey = keyPair.publicKey
```

This is very similar to the previous examples for generating RSA keys, such as *Sample 8.7*. The following are worth pointing out:

- In the dictionary that's passed as the first parameter, the value for the name key is 'RSASSA-PKCS1-v1_5' for calculating signatures with the PKCS#1 v1.5 padding. Alternatively, you can pass 'RSA-PSS' for PSS.

- Also, please note that the hashing algorithm that's used to calculate the signature is specified in the CryptoKey object, and it's defined in the dictionary using the hash key. Besides 'SHA-256', as shown in the previous example, other supported values include 'SHA-384', 'SHA-512', and 'SHA-1' (for compatibility with legacy applications).

- The usages array (the last parameter) contains the 'sign' and 'verify' values, which indicate that the key pair can be used to calculate and verify digital signatures, respectively.

Of course, you can also import external keys. For example, you may need to import another person's public key when you're verifying a digital signature. You can do that with the crypto.subtle.importKey() method, as we saw in *Chapter 7, Introduction to Cryptography in the Browser*, in the *Importing keys* section.

Once we have generated or imported a private key, we can then calculate the digital signature with the crypto.subtle.sign() method we introduced earlier.

For calculating signatures using the PKCS#1 v1.5, the value for the algorithm parameter that's passed to the method should be set like so:

```
const signature = await window.crypto.subtle.sign(
    {name: 'RSASSA-PKCS1-v1_5'},
    privateKey, message
)
```

However, if you're using PSS, the algorithm's parameter should be a dictionary similar to what's shown in this example:

```
const signature = await window.crypto.subtle.sign(
    {name: 'RSA-PSS', saltLength: 32},
    privateKey, message
)
```

Besides setting the algorithm's name, in this second case, we need to add a `saltLength` key that specifies the length of the salt to generate. The PKCS#1 v2 specification recommends setting this value to the length in bytes of the digest generated by the hashing function in use. For example, when it comes to using SHA-256 for calculating the digest of the message (as we did in *Sample 8.14*), the length of the digest and thus the recommended length of the salt for PSS is 32 (other values include 20 for SHA-1, 48 for SHA-384, and 64 for SHA-512).

The value of the `signature` object (once the promise has been resolved) is an `ArrayBuffer` object containing the raw bytes of the signature.

Using the public part of the key, we can validate the signature using the `crypto.subtle.verify()` method, as we introduced earlier:

```
const signatureValid = await window.crypto.subtle.verify(
    {name: 'RSASSA-PKCS1-v1_5'},
    publicKey, signature, message
)
```

The value of `signatureValid` (once the promise has been resolved) is a Boolean that indicates whether the signature is valid for the message.

Note that for PSS padding, you need to replace the first parameter with a dictionary like the one we used earlier: `{name: 'RSA-PSS', saltLength: 32}`.

In this book's GitHub repository, you can find a full example of calculating and verifying digital signatures in the `sign-rsa.js` file, in the `ch7-ch8-browser-cryptography` folder.

Calculating and verifying ECDSA signatures

As we saw in *Chapter 6*, *Digital Signatures with Node.js and Trust*, we can also use elliptic-curve cryptography to compute digital signatures using ECDSA and EdDSA, depending on the curve.

Support for **ECDSA** digital signatures, using the same curves we used for encryption (P-256, P-384, and P-512), is part of the WebCrypto standard. However, EdDSA is currently not implemented; should your application depend on that, you will need to look for third-party modules on npm.

To use ECDSA, the first step is to generate a new key pair or import an existing private or public key (please refer back to the previous chapter for importing keys, such as PEM-encoded ones). To generate a key pair, you can use the following code:

8.15: Generating a key pair for ECDSA (part of sign-ecdsa.js)

```
const keyPair = await window.crypto.subtle.generateKey(
    {name: 'ECDSA', namedCurve: 'P-256'},
    false, ['sign', 'verify']
)
const privateKey = keyPair.privateKey
const publicKey = keyPair.publicKey
```

This code sample is very similar to the one we used to generate an RSA key pair (see *Sample 8.14*), except for the `algorithm` parameter, which is a dictionary with two keys:

- name – the name of the algorithm – which is `'ECDSA'`.

- `namedCurve` indicates the name of the curve, following the NIST's nomenclature. As per the WebCrypto specification, we can use the same three curves that are supported for encryption/decryption for ECDSA: `'P-256'` (which we called prime256v1 in Node.js), `'P-384'`, and `'P-512'`.

Note that unlike with RSA keys, we don't define the hashing function when creating/importing the key object. Instead, that's set when we use the methods for signing or verifying.

To calculate an ECDSA digital signature, we can use the same `crypto.subtle.sign()` method we used for RSA, but with different options for the algorithm dictionary:

```
const signature = await window.crypto.subtle.sign(
    {name: 'ECDSA', hash: 'SHA-256'},
    privateKey, message
)
```

For the first parameter, we need to pass a dictionary containing two keys: the name of the algorithm, which is always `'ECDSA'` in this case, and the hashing function to use for calculating the digest of the message. The usual hashing functions are supported; that is, `'SHA-256'`, `'SHA-384'`, and `'SHA-512'`, plus `'SHA-1'` for compatibility reasons.

The result of the method is a promise that resolves with an `ArrayBuffer` containing the raw bytes of the signature.

Likewise, we can verify that an ECDSA signature is valid for a message with the `crypto.subtle.verify()` method. This function (asynchronously) returns a Boolean indicating whether the signature is valid or not:

```
const signatureValid = await window.crypto.subtle.verify(
    {name: 'ECDSA', hash: 'SHA-256'},
    publicKey, signature, message
)
```

Summary

In this chapter, we learned how to perform all the common cryptographic operations we've seen throughout this book in the context of a web browser, with JavaScript code that can be used on the client side. This included calculating digests with SHA-2 (and SHA-1); deriving keys and hashing passphrases with Argon2; encrypting and decrypting data using symmetric ciphers (AES), asymmetric ones (RSA), and hybrid schemes such as ECIES (based on ECDH); and calculating and verifying RSA and ECDSA digital signatures.

This chapter concludes both our exploration of cryptography in the browser and this book. I hope this book helped you learn about using cryptography in a practical way Armed with your newly acquired knowledge, I hope you'll be able to build applications that leverage common cryptographic operations and solutions to deliver better security and privacy to your users.

Thank you for reading, and happy coding!

Index

Packt.com

Subscribe to our online digital library for full access to over 7,000 books and videos, as well as industry leading tools to help you plan your personal development and advance your career. For more information, please visit our website.

Why subscribe?

- Spend less time learning and more time coding with practical eBooks and Videos from over 4,000 industry professionals

- Improve your learning with Skill Plans built especially for you

- Get a free eBook or video every month

- Fully searchable for easy access to vital information

- Copy and paste, print, and bookmark content

Did you know that Packt offers eBook versions of every book published, with PDF and ePub files available? You can upgrade to the eBook version at packt.com and as a print book customer, you are entitled to a discount on the eBook copy. Get in touch with us at customercare@packtpub.com for more details.

At www.packt.com, you can also read a collection of free technical articles, sign up for a range of free newsletters, and receive exclusive discounts and offers on Packt books and eBooks.

Other Books You May Enjoy

If you enjoyed this book, you may be interested in these other books by Packt:

Node.js Design Patterns

Mario Casciaro | Luciano Mammino

ISBN: 978-1-83921-411-0

- Become comfortable with writing asynchronous code by leveraging callbacks, promises, and the async/await syntax.

- Leverage Node.js streams to create data-driven asynchronous processing pipelines.

- Implement well-known software design patterns to create production grade applications

- Share code between Node.js and the browser and take advantage of full-stack JavaScript.

Burp Suite Cookbook

Natalie Sunny Marini-Wear

ISBN: 978-1-78953-173-2

- Configure Burp Suite for your web applications.
- Perform authentication, authorization, business logic, and data validation testing.
- Explore session management and client-side testing.
- Understand unrestricted file uploads and server-side request forgery.
- Execute XML external entity attacks with Burp.

Packt is searching for authors like you

If you're interested in becoming an author for Packt, please visit `authors.packtpub.com` and apply today. We have worked with thousands of developers and tech professionals, just like you, to help them share their insight with the global tech community. You can make a general application, apply for a specific hot topic that we are recruiting an author for, or submit your own idea.

Share Your Thoughts

Now you've finished *Essential Cryptography for JavaScript Developers*, we'd love to hear your thoughts! Scan the QR code below to go straight to the Amazon review page for this book and share your feedback or leave a review on the site that you purchased it from.

https://packt.link/r/1801075336

Your review is important to us and the tech community and will help us make sure we're delivering excellent quality content.

Printed in Great Britain
by Amazon

32925978R00123